Holy Spirit Driven!

When You're Spirit Driven,
All Heaven Breaks Loose!

POEMS

By
Edward J. Rishko, HSd

WestBow
PRESS®
A DIVISION OF THOMAS NELSON
& ZONDERVAN

WestBow Press books may be ordered through booksellers or by contacting:

WestBow Press
A Division of Thomas Nelson & Zondervan
1663 Liberty Drive
Bloomington, IN 47403
www.westbowpress.com
1 (866) 928-1240

ISBN: 978-1-5127-6983-8 (sc)
ISBN: 978-1-5127-6982-1 (e)

Library of Congress Control Number: 2016921302

Print information available on the last page.

WestBow Press rev. date: 01/25/2017

DISCLAIMER

The poems contained herein were wholly created by the author, except where noted. They reflect the author's personal inspired thoughts. No exact bible quotes were used except in one instance, and that reference is identified. All scripture has been paraphrased from memory, without specific reference to any particular bible version. The author has studied the New Revised Standard Version, the King James Bible, the New King James Bible, and the Scofield Study Bible (Containing the Authorized King James Version). Any combination of words in these poems, which may be exact quotes from any bible, is unknown to the author and is purely coincidental. If any are found, please contact the publisher in order that future publications can then give proper credit.

CONTENTS

PREFACE

This book is an improbable expression of how God worked in my life. It contains poems that I wrote with surprising ease. Being spontaneously creative is a skill I never thought I had. Come! Reminisce with me. Read how God worked in my life! Read entertaining and inspired poems containing God's wisdom.

When I surveyed my writings of the past fifteen years or so, I was shocked! How could I have written over eighty poems or songs? About fifty were within the last two years! I don't do this; I'm not that creative. I usually altered, amended, or otherwise critiqued what other people wrote. My degree is in mathematics, not English. I don't create! Or maybe, just maybe, I always possessed this creative skill, but I never realized it or was never encouraged to develop and hone it. Maybe I had received this gift when I was born again! 'Tis a puzzlement with a joyful allure! 'Tis a gift from God that I'm overjoyed to possess and share!

Let's start at the very beginning. Let me tell you a little bit about my background so that you'll better understand this improbable state in which I find myself today.

In eleventh grade at Old Forge High School in Old Forge, Pennsylvania, I wrote my first story. It was about my friend Pat and me and how we skipped school for a day. We went fishing about three miles away, over a low mountain west of town. We caught no fish, got rained on, caught colds, and missed a pop quiz. The story was a hit with my English teacher and principal. But regrettably, I never saw the potential that this short story might lead me to a career in writing or journalism, and I don't recall having been encouraged to pursue writing by anyone. I simply remember hearing "Attaboy, Ed!" from my family and friends.

Later that year, I wrote another story about my hero, my father. My dad had a sixth-grade education, but he could do virtually anything. He was a coal miner—a job he never wanted his sons to have. He was an auto mechanic. Mom told the story of how dad had bought his first car in the early 1930s, drove it home, took it apart, and put it back together again. He had a couple of parts left over, but he learned how the car was built and how it worked. Subsequently, dad could fix anything on cars. Dad was also a carpenter. He and our whole family built the house our family lived in when I was growing up; it was totally built by us from the ground up, including digging out the cellar by hand. In fact, the lumber used to build our house came from a house my uncle and dad had torn down from nearby Scranton. One summer, my cousin Butch, my boyhood chum, and I pulled broken, bent, and rusted nails from the lumber—not a fun summer job for teenage boys! The lumber was recycled into our house, which still stands today; my brother Rich still lives in it. In fact, our house telephone number has never changed since we got the number in the 1950s, with the exception of having had an area code added to it.

Financially, our family lived from paycheck to paycheck. Dad's usual Friday paycheck was used to pay rent and buy food and clothes. Whatever was leftover was used to buy something for the house as it was built over several years. Dad would get a door one week, a window the next, and then a sink. We never owed one penny on the house. What great examples of discipline my mom and dad were for us kids!

My dad's last job was working for Chamberlain Corp, which manufactured cannon shells for the military. He was responsible for maintaining the parts inventory for the company's equipment. Finally, my dad, known as Andy to his family and friends, could speak English, Polish, Russian, and a little bit of Yiddish. Wow, how great is that? How great was he? I appreciate that God had my hero living in my very own presence, to raise me with proper morals and values. Thanks, God!

However, to ignore my mom, would be a sin. Mom was the rock of our home. She was the faithful housewife, accountant, cook, and spiritual guidance counselor for all of us. As my wife, Nita, once commented to me after several years of being part of our family, mom was "General Mom." Whatever mom said, that was the way it was! She was a very strong person, who supplemented dad's income, at times, by working in local blouse or dress factories. She always kept our lives simple and focused on Jesus. Her philosophies were also simple. Of criminals: – they'll get theirs one day; always do what's right. On keeping up with the "Jones's:" – there are few such families; thank God for what you have. On work: – always do your best, —a biblical principal. Mom taught us contentment and happiness. Mom was also the best! (Thanks, mom; I know you hear this from heaven.) By the way, my mom's name was Anastasia, which I learned from a priest at her funeral service, that it means *resurrection* in Greek. Wow! I wish I had known that from my childhood!

This gives you some idea about my childhood environment. We were poor; we were blue collar through and through. Not one family member, on either mom's or dad's side, was in a profession or had ever gone to college. But we lived as God prescribed, or at least we tried our best to do so. We were rich in spirit, and God provided enough food, clothing, and shelter, as the Bible promises. For example, my typical lunch for school was a bologna sandwich. But many times I took cold pizza; for me, this was a treat, having Old Forge pizza at school and not in one of our town's many pizza parlors. (By the way, Old Forge claims to be the pizza capital of the world. I believe it!) On the opposite side of my culinary lunches was the time mom packed a pork and bean sandwich for me. Yuck! Oh, to have a bologna sandwich! Talk about a teenager's embarrassing moment in front of friends. This drove home the fact that dad's weekly paycheck was crucial to our lives. But I repeat: our family never lacked for any necessities. God always provided!

We lived in a house with caring, loving parents and siblings. In fact, my two brothers, Rich and Bill; our sister, Eleanor; and I are not only siblings but good friends as well. My sister has since passed; I miss her. God had blessed us abundantly with good, honest, God-fearing Roman and Greek Catholic and Russian Orthodox family members, including all my aunts, uncles, cousins, and grandparents. Thank You again, God.

I graduated from Wilkes College (now Wilkes University in Wilkes Barre) in 1966 with a BA in mathematics. I followed my big brother, Bill, five years my senior, who received his electrical engineering degree from Penn State, but he started one year before me at Wilkes. We were the first two from our entire family to attend college. Later on, several of our twenty-plus cousins earned college degrees. After graduation, I took my first professional job with the Defense Intelligence Agency (DIA) in the Arlington, Virginia, area. (The DIA is the Department of Defense's equivalent of the CIA.) That was when I left home at age twenty-two. I moved to and lived in Arlington and different northern Virginia towns for the next forty years.

Religiously, I was raised Roman Catholic. As such, I was born, circumcised, christened, and baptized in Garden City, Pennsylvania. I had my first Holy Communion and was confirmed in St. Stanislaus Roman Catholic Church in Old Forge. I married a Catholic woman when I was twenty-three, but I divorced her a year later—my worst life failure. This was almost fatal to me as a "good Catholic," and I knew I was destined for an eternity in hell. But God is good, and He would be merciful to me, as I would later find out!

How could I continue to live in the sin of divorce? I considered suicide, but to me, that was worse than divorce. With little support from my church, I suppressed my guilt and shame, figuring God didn't approve of me taking my own life. After all, I believed it was He who prevented me from committing suicide. I now know for sure I was right! Thank You, Father!

But God wasn't finished with me. Two years after my divorce, God sent me the most beautiful, wonderful Kentucky woman, and she filled a void in my life. Juanita was her name—Nita to everyone. Her background was eerily similar to mine: coal mining family; Christian (Baptist); and a poor, caring, loving, honest family. But what an accent! It took me a few trips to Hazard, Kentucky, her hometown, before I was finally able to understand everything being said in the hollers and hills there. In fact, my wife and her cousin Karen got great delight and laughter in hearing the ways I'd mispronounce the names of nearby towns. Take Beattyville, for example. It is pronounced "bay-tuh-vul." But I'm not going there! These two still chuckle when they occasionally hear me speak my unique dialect of Pennsylvania English, like when I say "I'll go wicha" instead of "I'll go with you," or "bachry" instead of "battery." But that's fodder for another book.

Both my wife and I worked at the DIA in Arlington, at Arlington Hall Station; that was where we met. A mutual friend from work, Marge Yelland, introduced us to each other. We needed a fifth person to complete our five-person bowling team, and Nita was that person. Interestingly, I taught Nita to bowl, and she taught me to ski. We lived, worked, bowled, and skied with fellow DIA employees. Because we worked in intelligence, we were part of a closely knit group of friends who would never discuss our work outside our office buildings. We married in 1970; attended Baptist churches; bore our son, Greg, in 1972; and attended church every week. However, as our son reached his teenage years, he refused to go to church without a fight. Regretfully, we let God slip from his life and ours, but we still lived "good" lives. Or so we thought!

Fast-forward some twenty-five years. Nita and I were now both retired, and we moved to Haymarket, Virginia, on the first mountain twenty-five miles due west of Washington D.C. There, from our dream retirement log home, we decided we needed to get God back into our lives. We did, and in a very big way! We joined Sudley United Methodist Church on the Civil War battlefield near Manassas.

We integrated back into a loving, caring Christian community of believers. It was a godsend. We thrived and studied the Bible extensively, taking four thirty-two-week disciple Bible study courses over four consecutive years. I even began to lead some of the classes—something I never thought I could do. But I did, or I should say, God enabled me to do. The courses gave me a greater sense of responsibility, to be sure that I accurately taught the Bible. I have almost become a zealot in my Bible reading and research, and I love it!

As I think back, when I started Bible study, it was the first time I'd owned or read a Bible. In fact, I never knew anyone back home in Pennsylvania who owned one. We learned our religious education at weekly catechism classes through high school. We also heard Bible stories read by priests during weekly Sunday masses. When I did read the Bible for myself, I came to realize I was familiar with most of its stories. Why was that? I later learned that churches preach most of the Bible stories according to a three-year liturgical cycle. Every three years, we'd hear most of the Bible in church. Finally, I owe much of my initial Bible training to my first Bible study teacher, Charlie French, at Sudley UMC. Charlie was a great teacher, and I learned much from him. Praise you, Charlie! Thank You, God!

One day Charlie asked me if I'd like to attend a weekend retreat called The Walk to Emmaus. This is similar to other Christian retreats, such as Cursillo, Chrysalis, Kairos, Journey, and others. It is a seventy-two-hour event that spans Thursday evening through Sunday evening. Charlie never told me exactly what it was, only that I would "see the face of Jesus." What an offer! How could I refuse? I didn't! So in November 2000, I went to the 4H Training Center, near Front Royal, Virginia, in the mountains for my Loudoun Valley Walk to Emmaus #31. It was awesome, life-changing, and out of this world! For me, it was the single most important thing I had ever done in my Christian life, and I was almost fifty-seven years old! It saved my soul.

The second most important life event for me was marrying Nita; we've now been married for forty-seven years. The third significant event was having our son, Greg. The fourth most significant event was moving to Florida to help raise our first grandson, Zachary.

Let me explain this fourth event. When Greg (raised Christian) married his first wife (raised Jewish), they informed us they intended to expose Zack to both Judaism and Christianity, and to let him decide which faith he would follow. Nita and I responded by deciding we'd have to move to Florida, if Zack were to have any chance of becoming a Christian. We sold our house in Virginia and moved to Port St. Lucie, Florida, to be near the three of them, who also lived there.

For us, this was a big deal. We had lived in northern Virginia for almost forty years. All our friends were there. We established ourselves into a very loving church family in nearby Manassas, Virginia. We were part of a large, fantastic Emmaus community of faithful believers. We lived in our fantastic log house, our "final" retirement home in the mountains. We were active in our civic association. From Virginia, we lived within equal driving distances to our families in Pennsylvania, Ohio, and Kentucky. Life was perfect for us, and God blessed us abundantly. We were living the life of Riley. We were living in paradise, a little corner of heaven in Virginia. How could we move? Why would we? But we did!

Never in my wildest dreams did I expect what God had in mind for Nita and me because of this. We sacrificed everything for our grandson's sake. Now here we are, some twelve years later, and we're part of another loving church family with a good Emmaus community. We have a nice house and have helped raise not one but two wonderful grandsons, Zack and Jacob. From my perspective, God continued to bless us because we did what He wanted us to do. He moved us from one part of paradise in Virginia to a very different part of paradise in Florida. Although I still miss the fall colors, crisp winter air, and occasional snows of Virginia, we don't regret the move. God has blessed us even more here! Living in Virginia was wonderful, but helping raise two grandchildren in Florida is priceless.

My Emmaus weekend was life-changing. It was there that God revealed to me just how good, forgiving, and loving He is! Combining this with our decision to move to Florida, we thank Him for His continued blessings upon our family and me, especially for how He's filled me with His Holy Spirit to serve Him.

Why do I say this? Let me explain this Holy Spirit thing by backtracking to my Walk to Emmaus. On that weekend, late Saturday evening, I confessed and repented of my sins, and I surrendered my life to Jesus Christ. Afterward, we retired for the night. Then very early Sunday morning, on November 5, 2000, it happened—something I call my biblical experience!

1. God spoke to me!
2. God called me by my name!
3. God forgave me my worst sins!

First and foremost, He forgave my divorce sin! He literally said, "Ed, remember when you divorced your first wife? You're forgiven. Forget it."

I wept uncontrollably with great tears of joy as I sang the many songs we learned that weekend. The little black cloud that had hung over my head for some thirty two years, and that occasionally reared its ugly head, was gone forever!

Then, God spoke to me two more times in like manner, and He forgave me the two other worse sins I had committed. I could not contain myself and wept uncontrollably! I felt like I was airborne, like I was floating!

Afterward, I pondered the things that happened to me, and guess what? I had come to the realization that I had been born again! Hallelujah! Thank You, God. Thank You! My guilt and shame were gone! I'd never felt so free in all my life! I felt and knew exactly what Dr. Martin Luther King Jr. meant when he said in his famous speech at the Lincoln Memorial, "Free at last! Free at last! Thank God Almighty, I'm free at last!" I had been freed from the oppression of sin and the lies of the deceiver, the devil, Satan. Thank You, God! Thank You again!

I left that retreat weightless; my feet never touched the ground. I was flying really high! As I left, I recalled Luke 7:47, which says, "He who is forgiven little, loves little." For me, the converse was true: "He who is forgiven more, loves more." And boy, was I ever forgiven more! God is very good indeed!

In John 14:15, God says, "If you love me, keep my commands." How can I but obey my Lord, who relieved the guilt and shame that I'd harbored in my mind for thirty two years? How much does God love a sinner like me? Just as much as He loves a sinner like you! I finally learned the lesson of Romans 2:4: "the goodness of God leads one to repentance." Oh, what goodness God bestowed upon me that morning. If God did this for me, he can certainly do it for you!

After one completes his Walk to Emmaus, he joins a weekly reunion group, which is to hold each other accountable for their Christian lives. Each day after the walk is called a fourth day. Since my walk in November 2000, I have never regressed from my Virginia mountain high—no offense to John Denver. I can do nothing less than glorify my King and lead others to Him every fourth day of my life. I can do no less. God had saved me from hell. He pulled me from the burning fire, and He has prepared a room for me in the new Jerusalem to be with Him forever. I'm not worthy, God, but thank You again for your gifts of salvation and eternal life with You! There is no other like You.

"God is good, all the time. All the time, God is good!" We've all heard this before, and we've heard this Christian hymn: "Jesus loves me this I know, for the Bible tells me so. Little ones to Him belong. We are weak but He is strong. Yes, Jesus loves me! Yes, Jesus loves me! Yes, Jesus loves me! The Bible tells me so."*

* Written by Anna Bartlett Warner

The Bible tells us that if we confess and repent our sins, believe Jesus is the Son of God, and believe He died for our sins, then we will be saved. I know these words are true because God saved me through them. I am, no doubt, a new creation!

This book is my testimony of how, when I finally listened to the Holy Spirit, He filled my heart and mind with great words of God's wisdom. Most of my poems are in response to reading scripture and being led to write what the Holy Spirit told me. In virtually every instance, each poem was written within forty-five minutes of when I started it. Usually the urge to write them came as I finished reading my Bible. Only sometimes did I sit down and decide that I wanted to write a poem about some other specific topics; these usually took longer to compose. Regardless, I contend that the Holy Spirit inspired my every word. How awesome is that?

I now believe that I thoroughly understand what it means that all scripture is "God-breathed" (2 Tim 3:16) or Holy Spirit driven (HSd). Men who wrote the bible didn't write scripture using their own imagination; they were merely the Spirit's scribes. I, likewise, contend that I am merely God's scribe.! But it simply took me a very long route to get to the place in my life where I realized it. Yes,! God is good! No,! God is great!!!! Hallelujah!

Since beginning this book, I read another book, *Mathematics Proves Holy Scripture*, by Karl Sabiers, M.A., copyright 1941 and renewed in 1969. It expands upon the efforts of Dr. Ivan Panin, a Russian mathematician, who spent 50 years of his life studying the Bible in the original Greek and Hebrew languages. He discovered hundreds of unbelievably amazing and phenomenal relationships. He found, for example, that the chance of 24 biblically independent mathematical features occurring by chance is 1 in 191 quadrillion! That is 1 in 191 followed by 18 zeroes. THIS BOOK PROVIDES INDISPUTABLE PROOF THAT NO HUMAN BEINGS COULD HAVE POSSIBLY WRITTEN THE BIBLE! WOW! Let me repeat: THIS BOOK PROVIDES INDISPUTABLE PROOF THAT NO HUMAN BEINGS COULD HAVE POSSIBLY WRITTEN THE BIBLE! I believe every human being on earth should read this book and Ivan Panin's writings. They will, without a doubt, change their opinion about the nature of the Bible being true and that it is God's inerrant word!

All of this knowledge reinforces my testimony, as a mathematician, that God loves us. That Jesus loves us! That the Holy Spirit loves us! And you, my reader, are one of us! If you've not come to Jesus, come today! He is waiting for you.

My greatest hope is that at least one person reading these poems will come to realize the goodness of God, as well as the extreme importance and absolute necessity of accepting Jesus Christ as his or her Lord and Savior and receiving eternal life through Him.

In the meantime, sit back, relax, and enjoy the poems. May the God of creation guide you into His presence, in Jesus' name!

DEDICATION

I dedicate this book to God and to my loving wife, Juanita, whom God sent into my life when I was in my deepest valley of despair. I had been divorced from my first wife and was a psychological mess. Nita's and my mutual backgrounds instantly resonated with each other, and with her love, compassion, and alluring Southern accent, she helped bring me back to my fun-loving, happy, contented self—and into God's presence.

Nita and I bonded immediately. We became close friends and bowling and skiing partners. We grew closer until God brought us together in holy matrimony. Thank You, God! We now stay close together in God's word.

She accepted me as I was: a broken, aching man who needed restoration. To me, a divorced Catholic, this was huge. She helped restore me. She believed in me. She helped me grow into the mature, secure person I have become. Next to Jesus, she is my rock. Without her, I don't know where I might be today. Certainly I would not have had my faith restored or become the success she thinks I am.

Nita, I love you. Thanks for hanging with me through thick and thin. Thank you for trusting in me. You are the best! As our grandson Jacob would say, "Seriously!" Next to God, Nita, you are my sunshine!

That said, I give God my greatest thanks. It was very early one morning, about 4:00 a.m., when God spoke to me. I was sitting in my living room chair and reading my Bible. I closed it and laid it on my lap. I looked at it. I thought to myself, "This is the Word of God." And if it's the Word of God then I should be able to hear it. I put it up to my right ear. I then heard God tell me, "I love you. I want you to spend eternity with Me. Love one another. Live like Jesus lived." Wow! God, our Creator, literally spoke to me just like He spoke to Moses! Yes, Father, I joyfully dedicate this book to You! I can do no less than honor You with these works, which the Holy Spirit had me write. Thank You, thank You, thank You!

IN APPRECIATION

I wholeheartedly thank Debbie Cogswell, one of "God's Holy Band of Thieves," (read the poem) who diligently edited this book for me. She is the only person I know who reads *everything* in a book: book jackets, ISBN number, publisher, copyright date, preface—every single word! She did a great job. Thanks, Debbie!

I also thank each of my church family members who have heard or read some of my poems and encouraged me to do more. You will never know how much I appreciate you. I love all y'all! May God be "wicha" always!

And last but really first, I thank God for His proddings and callings. If not for His love, grace, mercy, compassion, forgiveness, and direction, this book would have never been written. As it is, I thank the Holy Spirit for leading my mind and fingers to compose and write what He led me to write. After all, this book of poems is Holy Spirit driven (HSd).

WHEN TWO HEARTS KISS*

Why is it so, when Christians meet?
We hug a lot! 'Tis how we greet!

Upon such hugs, we Christians feed.
How wonderful, this simple deed!

For when we do each other hug,
Within our hearts we feel a tug,

A gentle pull of hearts that yearn
To share our love this need does burn.

Our hearts are warmed to show we care,
And with old friends we need to share.

For we know each hug uplifts.
'Tis God designed these perfect gifts.

Great gifts He sends between just two.
His presence felt in each of you.

Arms outstretched, someone to hold.
Joyful smiles, two bodies enfold.

How nice to feel this mild embrace,
Sharing love, and feeling God's grace!

So when one chest does touch another,
You feel God's love, that's like no other.

When next you greet, remember this:
A hug is when two hearts kiss.

---

* This poem was published by Eber & Wein in *Beyond the Sea: Homecoming*.
It was chosen in a *Parade* magazine contest in 2015—my first published poem.

MARY'S LAMB

Mary had a little Lamb. His soul was white as snow.
And everywhere the Lamb had gone, He let the people know.

God's kingdom has come down to earth in the form of God's great Son:
Jesus Christ of virgin birth, Messiah, the anointed one.

Know that God, our Father, had sent to earth this Son
With salvation that He offers to each and every one.

How simple, He does tell us, to end all worry and strife!
Believe that Jesus died for you. You'll gain eternal life!

How wonderful this promise! How awesome such good news!
Ponder the Gospel's truthfulness and know God's calling you.

Earnestly read the Bible. Discover eternal life is true!
The evidence is overwhelming. Believe it—you'll know what to do.

Jesus died and was resurrected. Hundreds saw this with their eyes.
So come to Jesus before it's too late! Stop believing Satan's lies!

Remember that God loves us, and each person will He save
Who believes His "foolish" message and avoids the final grave.

The "foolish" words are simple: believe Jesus died for you.
Believe with all your heart, and bask in life anew.

So tarry not, for time is short 'til Lord Jesus returns again.
The Lion of Judah is how He'll come, the one born as the Lamb.

THAT SPECIAL GLOW

No longer do I live for me. My life is not my own.
My Savior Jesus cleansed me and prepared for me a home.

I have yielded and surrendered my body, heart, and soul
To the one who gives us life, to the one we seek to know.

Oft times I thought I was saved, but little did I know
Until I surrendered to Christ, I would not have that special glow.

That special glow the Spirit gives as He pours into us God's love,
That special glow when we're born again and blessed by God above!

"I once was lost, but now I'm found." I've heard it said before.
I thought I was *always* a Christian, but I was really behind the door.

Yes, I was christened and baptized too, confirmed and thought I knew.
A born-again Christian I had *always* been, 'til I surrendered and my heart flew.

Oh, what glory my soul beheld as Jesus, opened the door!
He called my name and forgave my sins, saying, "I remember them no more."

As the door closed behind us, it was very clear, and I knew
I became a new creation, the kind of a heavenly brew.

Full of love and life am I, relieved of my burden and shame,
Joyful and ever thankful, never looking back again.

My heart has been flying since that early November morn.
That special glow within my heart is proof that I am reborn.

The light of my soul that you see in me will ever shine so brightly,
For it's really the light of Jesus, which He renews in my heart nightly!

So, now I live for Jesus Christ to pass on His great gift,
To help others come to the light; their burdens He will lift.

To give them great relief and joy; their futures etched in stone,
Knowing with full assurance Jesus is their final home.

"Come to Jesus now!" now I say. "God's every promise heed.
Surrender to His majesty, and on joy and love you will feed."

Amen!

COME TO ME

Come to Me! Come to Me!
I love you so. Please come to Me.
Live forever. Come to Me.
I am God. Please, come to Me.

I sent my Son, Lord Jesus Christ.
He paid the price, this Jesus Christ.
He will redeem, Lord Jesus Christ.
You will be worthy in Jesus Christ.

Turn from your sin, and live My way.
Read My words. Please live My way.
Deny yourself—the only way.
Live like Jesus, no other way.

No sin's too great that I won't forgive.
When you confess, I shall forgive.
There is no doubt; I always forgive.
Come to Me; forever live.

What do I hear, Lord Jesus Christ?
A confession to My Jesus Christ!
One more soul for Jesus Christ!
Another surrendered to Jesus Christ!

Hallelujah! You've been redeemed!
Hallelujah! You've been made clean.
Gone is your guilt. You're void of shame.
You've been saved in Jesus' name.

Now angels sing another's saved
For the God from the once depraved.
As Jesus opens wide the door,
Have joy and peace forevermore!

GOD'S WISDOM*

Read God's Holy Bible; treasure His commands.
Cry out for discernment; seek to understand.
Then the God of heaven, His fear you'll come to know.
For the Lord gives wisdom to save you from your foe.

Wisdom makes you happy and gives you longer life,
Fills you with great courage to deal with every strife!
Trust in God for wisdom, and read His words each day.
He'll be right there with you, to safely guard your way

God's knowledge is so pleasant when wisdom fills your heart,
As you discern what's evil and watch all threats depart.
Do not walk in darkness or leave righteousness behind.
That's the path to death; pain and suffering there you'll find.

From Your words, God, let us know. Take us where we yearn to go.
Have Your words to us indwell; to heaven, guide us 'way from hell.
God is love. God is life. Give us wisdom; end our strife.
You, O God, are in control. Heal our hearts and save our souls.

---

* **Inspired by Psalms 1-3.**

DOUBT NOT

Some people say that God is dead; His Word they don't believe.
They have fallen to the trap that Satan did conceive.

Satan's the greatest of deceivers. He roams the world throughout,
Using all his power and might to place in us great doubt.

For doubting is his major tool; he uses it with skill.
His purpose is so very clear: he wants our souls to kill.

When we doubt God's holy word, we question what is truth,
And believing is impossible; our hearts we cannot soothe.

Remember what God said to Eve about the fruit of that one tree?
Did God surely say you would die? Do eat and be like He!

So God's first two believed the lie, and of the fruit they ate.
And as their eyes were opened wide, they realized their fate.

God was displeased with both of them; from the garden He cast them out.
And since the time of that first sin, man has been cursed to live in doubt.

But God, He has a greater plan to bring us back to Him.
He sent His Son, named Jesus Christ, to pay for all our sin.

He tells us to believe in Christ, the Son of God by name,
The one who died for all our sins to relieve our guilt and shame!

But Satan knows his time is short. His plan did Jesus kill,
And the only hope he has is to have us doubt God's will.

But God says that He loves us all. He wants no one to die.
Believe, and you will always live in mansions in the sky.

He tells us we are kings and priests when Jesus is our Lord.
As kings we have authority, with power o'er all the world.

At Jesus' name, all demons flee; they shudder at His name.
Disease and illness cease to be. To sickness no power came.

He tells us to believe, not doubt, when in Jesus' name we ask.
Believe we have received it, and in His glory we shall bask!

"Why?" you ask. "How do you know that God is really there?"
I know 'cause He's forgiven me and removed my every care.

He called me by first name; my worst sins He cast away!
Guilt and shame, once in my heart, now have no place to stay.

Great joy I felt when grace I received. My soul was filled with delight.
I burst out in song on that cold eve. I knew I'd been touched by the light.

As I gazed into the sky, the stars seemed so much brighter.
My feet, they did not touch the floor; my body felt much lighter.

I felt a glow within my heart, so sweet and full of love.
I knew I had been born again, blessed by my God above.

Now I do not worry, or fret or cry or yearn.
My God cares so much for me; for Him does my heart burn.

I know that it's God's Spirit that now lives in my heart,
Filling me with God's love. From it I'll never part.

Now I am so happy I never will go back.
The sad life that I led was not on the right track.

How does one explain why I'm so joyful every day?
Is it not the hand of God, just as in Jesus' day?

Yes, I say. Just like the twelve, my testimony is strong.
My loving God came down to me; for His presence did I long!

How can one not want to shout; how can one not scream,
When our Creator speaks to you and it's not in a dream?

God is alive! God is not dead! Myself, I heard Him speak!
I'll profess this to the end! He makes me strong, not weak.

In whom do you now place your trust? Our God, or that deceiver?
Know God keeps His every word. I know—I'm a believer.

Remember Christ's first disciples, who saw Jesus dead, then alive.
Most, they died attesting this. Why would they die if it was a lie?

No! They knew the truth: *Jesus Christ is alive.*
They lived to tell the world, and as Christians they did thrive.

Remember, God loves us all and wants no one to die.
Trust in Him! Cast out your doubt; then you will know why!

Why does the world live in doubt with so much death and pain?
That's been Satan's plan all along, 'til Jesus comes again.

But you can have God's peace right now. Trust in Him, don't doubt.
Read His word, believe in Him, and you'll never do without.

SEEKING PEACE

We live a lie each day, and peace to us unknown.
We seek something brand-new, another thing to own.

Or maybe what we want is people to know our name!
Surely we'll be happy when raised aloft in fame.

But somehow we still search for something that we lack.
Things and fame mean nothing, 'cause we keep coming back.

Coming back unfilled, our hearts still feel so sad.
What can still be missing? What can make us glad?

Why is it when our goal we reach, we very often fret?
That which we so longed for, we quickly do forget.

What is this thing we do? Why are we not content?
Why are we not happy? Our thinking, is it bent?

Where do we turn to find the answer to this quest?
Where does true wisdom lie? Which way to go is best?

The answer is so simple when we look unto the Lord.
His scripture's there to guide us; now, read His every word.

God tells us that He loves us and cares for all in need.
He's reaching out to us right now, so come to Him and feed.

Our sins He will forgive us; compassion is His glory.
He'll remember them no more. Let's join Him in His story.

He'll fill us with great joy; He'll be always at our side.
He'll be our friend forever. His arms are open wide!

If we truly want peace, it's there for God to give.
Submit to His Son, Jesus, and forever with Him live.

Then we will be happy! God's peace He will provide.
Content we'll be forever. No blessings will He hide!

JOYFUL GIVING

You are worthy; we are not. You give us everything we got.
We give You thanks and gifts and praise, as we struggle to live these days.

We serve the sick, we serve the blind, to live like Jesus and be kind.
We feed the hungry one and all, yet do we answer when God calls?

Lord, it seems we lack each day the means to live it in Your way.
Our food is sparse; the rent is due. If we give more, can we make due?

My precious child, God loves you so. His mercy abounds more than you know.
He sent us Jesus to give us life that you may live with little strife.

That's how much He cares for you. He gave His Son's life to get you through.
Abundant life to believers all! So trust and beckon to God's call.

Remember the fish and loaves of bread, and the crowds that Jesus fed.
Does this not show God's power indeed? Those coming to Him, He will feed!

Have faith in God and have no fear. Trust and give with joy and cheer.
When it's God's will you do in deed, he'll satisfy your every need.

So come to the throne of God's great grace; your fears and worries He will erase.
Smile with joy! Lay down your gift. He'll bless you more, and your spirit uplift.

Remember: Giving is *not* a matter of money. It is a matter of one's faith, trust, and commitment to God. It is a biblical principle that the more one gives willingly to God, the more one gets to give to God.

Do Not Hide or Run Away

God is everywhere. There is no place to hide.
From His love, grace, and mercy, He wants in us to abide.

He is pursuing us to save us from the pit.
Only through God's efforts are we saved, *not by our wit*.

We must be very careful; God's love is infinite.
But because He's also just, un-forgiven sin leads to the pit.

Know that God loves sinners and wants them to repent.
Only if they confess and turn, to the pit they won't be sent.

So is God's love unconditional, or does He want us clean?
Will He allow anyone impure in His presence to be seen?

No, I say, nothing unclean is allowed into His view.
Think of your life and of your sins. What would He think of you?

Remember, no one is righteous—no, not anyone.
Earnestly repent and confess; then to Him He'll let you come.

Give your repentant, broken heart to Jesus in humbleness.
Then He'll set your heart straight, and your life He'll greatly bless.

Please, come to Jesus—submit to Him! His love will lift you up!
You'll bask in peace and love and joy overflowing from His cup.

So do not hide or run away; God wants you as His friend.
Let Him come into your heart before your time on earth does end.

GOD'S SILENT SHOUTS

Look around and listen; hear the silent shouts of God.
Heard from His creation, the universe so broad.

For when God spoke the words, He made a giant clock.
Quadrillions of new worlds sustained by God's own Rock!

The size of heaven above is many light-years across.
Beauty beyond compare tainted only by the cross!

Earth first, then came heaven, to clothe God's precious work.
Precise and delicate, no accident or mindless quirk!

For God unrolled the heavens; 'twas not a great big bang!
Set it all in motion! God's sign of greatness rang!

His message is sublime, one that screams and yells.
Just like the voiceless cross its silent story tells.

So too the universe, orderly and precise!
Intelligently designed, not by chance or dice.

One circuit across the skies, it moves by God's own word!
One thousand years they pass, but as one day to the Lord!

Man's science does attest this cycle to be true.
Can't you hear God shouting? 'Tis one great sign to you!

Next look at planet earth for man, God's masterpiece.
Beauty beyond compare, complex beyond our reach!

Consider every detail in our biosphere of life.
But without earth's bright sun, would be just a rock in strife.

Consider life itself and the law of biogenesis.
Life only begets life, God tells us in Genesis.

Fish, fowl, beast, and human—each one God brought to life.
Scientists can't do this; their efforts end in strife.

Not one can explain life and from whence it did begin.
A singularity they think, they guess to be its origin.

In this the laws of physics, on earth they're not the same.
From this lame assertion, they weave their web of shame.

Upon this wild assumption, many theories they do make.
But from God's words of wisdom, their falsehoods they can't shake.

For none has ever proved any word from God a lie.
They close their intellectual minds, denying one day they'll die.

Can't you hear God shouting? See the marvel in a man?
How incredibly complex! Evolved without a plan?

Which came first to be? Heart, lungs, blood, or eye?
To those with common sense, all were created in one try.

Without blood or mouth or brain, or carotid artery,
No man could live without any one—a man he would not be.

Listen to the buzzing of bees as they fly about,
Pollenating plants—is this not another God shout?

For had God made no bees, no plant could propagate.
Synergistic life we have; this need God did create.

Isn't this another shout? God's handiwork abounds!
Closing our eyes to such facts can deny none of God's sounds.

Most of all, we have God's words—each whisper, shout, and song,
Recorded in sixty-six books of the ages, none of which is proved wrong.

It tells of ancient times, of people, prophets, and things to come.
God told them what would happen, and what He told them had been done.

He told of virgin birth, how the Son of God would come,
Hundreds of years before it happened; from this fact, none could run.

He also said this Jesus would die upon a tree;
He'd pay the ransom price—the cost to set us free.

Three days and three nights later, He rose up from the grave.
Resurrected by the Father, Who did this for us to save.

Hundreds saw the resurrected Lord and swore that it was true.
Many died for this belief, but live eternal life anew.

Can't you hear God shouting? God wants you to come to Him!
Throw off the chains of fear and doubt. He'll eagerly let you in.

For the shouting only stops when the scales fall from your mind,
And your heart feels God's compassion—the feeling of a different kind.

When you come to realize the goodness God bestows,
Peace and love comes to repentant sinners; this every Christian knows.

They know to surrender their broken hearts in humbleness and shame,
And smile as the shouting stops and songs from heavenly choirs came!

Finally, you see it all: the magnificence of God's creation.
Now you want to shout it out in each and every nation.

Can't you hear God shouting yet? Oh, it's you—you're born again!
Now you're out doing God's bidding, saving others from the lion's den.

The silent shouts of God, you must help others understand.
You start by explaining God's universe and why it is so grand.

You then go and tell others how our awesome God's so good.
'Cause only when they realize this, will they choose Jesus 'cause they could.

Einstein said, "Logic can get one from point A to point B.
Imagination can get you anywhere"—anywhere you want to be.

But the Gospel can get you to Jesus, and Jesus gets you life eternal.
It's the great message of the ages; it's so grand and so supernal!

So ponder God's sun, moon, and stars in all their majesty.
Begin by shouting of God's greatness, though booming silence you only see!

Can't you hear God shouting? It's in everything you see.
Listen with your heart and soul until God says, "Come to Me!"

IN THE VALLEYS WE GROW

Sometimes life seems hard to bear,
Full of sorrow, trouble, and woe!
It's then we have to remember
It's in the valleys we grow.

If we stayed upon mountaintops
And never experienced pain,
We'd never appreciate God's true love;
We'd be living our lives in vain.

We have so much to learn from God;
Our growth seems very slow.
Sometimes we're on mountaintops,
But it's through valley trials we grow.

We do not always understand
Why things happen as they do.
But of one thing I'm very sure:
Our Lord will see us through.

Each valley comes to nothing,
Compared to Jesus on the cross.
He went through the valley of death;
His victory was Satan's loss.

Now He's King of the universe,
Will soon reign from Mount Zion on high.
He conquered death, and so could we.
Repent, believe, and you won't die.

Forgive me, Lord, for complaining
When I sometimes feel very low.
Just give me a gentle reminder
That it's in the valleys we grow.

Continue, Lord, to strengthen me
And to use my life each day
To share Your love with others,
And to help them find their way.

Thank You for the valleys, Lord,
Where pain and sufferings I know.
The mountaintops are glorious,
But it's in the valleys we grow.

Hide, Run, and Deny

You can't hide from God's love. You can't run from His grace.
You can't deny God's mercy. But you can hide from His face.

You can deny God's existence and all evidence ignore.
You can sincerely believe this and be wrong unto your core.

You can say you never saw Him in your life in any year.
Have you ever thought He loves you and yearns to bring you near?

Have you ever felt His presence in the complacency of your peace,
When you lived without a worry, when your guilt and pain did cease?

How often have you yearned, to know that God loves you,
But your heart somehow rejected this poignant point of view?

Why would God ever come to me? I'm unworthy—from Him must run!
It makes no sense He'd call me. Why would He ask *me* to come?

God loves you! Yes, He does! Wants none to perish, not one.
But we must accept His gift: the sin sacrifice of His Son.

Yes, this Jesus died for you! He died for sinners everyone!
Just take this gift and thank Him, and to you Jesus will come.

'Cause you're no worse than others who ever walked this earth.
There is not one who's worthy! Of righteousness there's a dearth!

So do not hide, run, or deny! God's truth will set you free!
His love, He's reaching out to you. Accept it; come and see.

GOD'S LADDER*

Rejoice and pray; give thanks! God tells us this to do.
When each of us obeys, He draws closer to you.

"Rejoice and pray; give thanks" are rungs on which you climb.
Abandon your old self; leave every sin behind!

Rejoice and pray; give thanks! You start to feel God's grace.
How wonderful the peace, eschew man's sinful race.

Rejoice and pray; give thanks! Climb unto the Lord!
Feast upon God's message! Digest His every word!

Rejoice and pray; give thanks! A gift He has for you.
Regardless if you're Gentile, no matter if you're Jew!

Rejoice and pray; give thanks! Eternal life He gives.
Remembers not your sins; those He all forgives.

Rejoice and pray; give thanks! God's love you now embrace.
Give your heart to Him; your sins He shall erase.

Rejoice and pray; give thanks! Do this every day.
Climb God's holy ladder. Please Him every way.

Rejoice and pray; give thanks! You almost see His face.
As you climb each rung, He extends to you more grace.

Rejoice and pray; give thanks! He sees your journey's true.
Your faith in Him is solid, the faith in Him you grew.

Rejoice and pray; give thanks! God's will, this is for you.
He will then sanctify you; when it's His will you do.

Rejoice and pray; give thanks! You've climbed God's ladder of love.
Journey's complete! Now glorify Him from your mansion high above!

---

* Inspired by 1 Thessalonians 5:16–18.

THE CROSS, THE CROSS

The cross, the cross! What does it mean? Where do we start the story?
Is this the way our awesome God, planned for us to share His glory?

At first we think about the Christ, how He suffered and died for us.
His sacrifice, His priceless gift that overcame our sin and fuss.

Think about eternal life and ask, "Is that God's goal?"
To live with Him and not in hell, which burns much hotter than coal!

Do we believe that heaven and hell are eternal places we'll live?
Or do we think at death we cease—endless life no one can give?

"So what?" we think. There is no proof that life goes on forever.
"Let's take the chance and live our way. We know our way is better."

'Cause if we do, and we are wrong and hell's a very real place,
We'll live in pain and shame alone, without relief, in disgrace!

The cross, the cross! It had to come; the world is full of sin.
For God wants us to live with Him, but no sinner is let in.

Think hard, we must! Consider this: our calendar's based on Him.
The Son of God, the Son of man, Jesus died for our sin!

Many saw Him dead then alive, and unto heaven taken up.
They swore the story to be true; they died drinking the martyr's cup.

Also, consider all ancient books; they refer to Jesus alive!
But if a lie, how could it be that such a story would ever thrive?

Today, billions believe in Jesus, whose lives He's totally changed.
This attests to the awesome truth—or is each one of them deranged?

Fool billions of the people all the time? Is this the morbid truth?
Or have they succumbed to Jesus and their aching lives He's soothed?

The cross, the cross! God sent His Son to pay for every sin.
No man could do this on his own; salvation he can't win.

Remember Jesus' disciples and how they died attesting to this story.
Think they would willingly die for a lie and face deaths so gory?

Or look at this another way. Lord, liar, lunatic—which is He?
These are the only three choices, and only one will set *you* free.

Could He fool so many for three long years of time?
If He was a fool or crazed, how could He be sublime?

How could He preach and teach and heal, if He was not the Lord?
'Cause thousands flocked to hear Him and hoped to be healed by His word!

Yes, the crowds followed Jesus; they went everywhere He went.
Were all these people deluded, or did they know He was heavenly sent?

The cross, the cross! "'Tis finished!" He cried, gave up the ghost and died.
But three days later, He arose triumphant. Then all knew He never lied.

Contemplate His miracles, the ones He performed each day.
Too many to call coincidences; He was showing us God's glorious way.

No, He's not a lunatic for calling Himself God, as He said,
Or for teaching scribes and scholars—is this a man whose mind is dead?

Look at ancient prophecies where God told us what would be.
That atonement would be made for our sins by this man from Galilee.

Our gracious God loved us so much; He saw man's sin was great.
And because we are His creations, only He could change our state.

So God the Father sent God the Son, for only God could bear the pain.
Then Jesus Christ obeyed, bled, and died to wash away our stain.

The cross, the cross! It is the heart of God's salvation story.
In this way, our awesome God planned for us to share His glory!

Come to Jesus today!

WHY DO WE GO TO CHURCH?

Why do we go to church? What do we seek to find?
Is something missing from our hearts, or something from our minds?
The answer to these questions is found in God's great plan.
To want to know our Maker abounds in every man.

Off to church we go, for surely God is there.
We feast on words of wisdom that show He really cares.
We hear God sent His Son to relieve our guilt and shame.
He tells us we are worthy. No condemnation to us came!

Salvation, we are also told, is there for every man
Who comes to Jesus Christ, though at first from Him we ran.
We find our loving God is full of mercy without end.
Greater than all our sin, and to all He does extend.

So lift your broken spirit; feast on God's great hope.
As long as you are living, He's there to help you cope.
No! More than cope with life, God will give you life anew.
Full of joy and peace and love—it's this He offers you.

Surrender to His Majesty; repent of every sin.
He'll forgive you and forget, then cleanse your heart within.
What a message! Is it true? When to Jesus I submit,
Eternal life He'd give me, and save me from the pit?

This gospel seems so simple. In it can one believe?
When we commit to Jesus, our iniquities He'll relieve.
See the joyous Christians; feel their love and peace within.
Would I be just as happy if Jesus forgives my sin?

Such wonderful words of comfort, they tug at me to start
A journey home to heaven, to fill the void in my heart!
Excitement fills my mind as God's words begin to stir.
As I hear His gentle whispers and my soul begins to purr.

I know I must now choose and decide how I shall live.
Do I follow Jesus, my heart to Him do give?
For when we do, God says that He will never leave us.
He'll prepare for us a room where we'll ever live with Jesus.

Why do we go to church? The answer is now clear:
To remind us that God loves us, and He wants us to be near.
Yes, I say all this is true; at church you'll find good news!
Live in joy, accept God's grace when Jesus you do choose.

SAINTS OR SINNERS?

We heard the greet: "Good morning, saints."
And all replied, "Good morning to you."
But then we heard, "Good morning, sinners."
"Good morning!" we all said too.

Are we saints, or are we sinners?
This makes no sense! How can it be?
Either we're saved and do not sin,
Or we sin and from God we flee!

Not so fast; 'tis not so simple.
We do not sin; we have God's grace.
We're born again, please realize;
This lesson learned you must embrace!

We're under God's grace, not under His law,
And without law, there's no sin.
Amazing grace through God the Son,
Salvation did each saint win.

But what about when we do slip,
And displease God in some way?
Does He hold this not against us
And turn His face away?

No! I say He knows our hearts,
That we, saved, belong to Him.
He knows we seek things from above;
It's our bodies which do sin.

Sin nature God sees in every one,
The source of sin, guilt, and shame.
Christians though are spirit led;
Condemnation God does restrain.

Remember—God does not forsake us
When sometimes we may stumble.
Confess, repent, and be assured;
You're still saved but must stay humble.

So are we saints, or are we sinners?
The answer is now clear.
We are saints in sinners' bodies,
Saved by grace, bereft of fear!

WALK TO EMMAUS
A Journey to Eternal Life

What is this Walk to Emmaus? What happens when you go?
You can't describe it easily; only those who went do know.

Listen to their very words, from their own lips they did come.
Then you won't want to walk there—you will want to run.

We learned that our God loves us and that we're not alone.
He deems us very worthy, and our hearts from us He'd won.

We learned that we should love more and be open to His call,
To spread the word about Him and of His gift for all.

Our fears we faced that weekend, and no one put us down.
The love shown us was awesome as smiles replaced our frowns.

God's love abounded everywhere as angels cared for us.
Little presents we received; we wondered what's the fuss.

As each day passed and the next began, our hearts began to glow.
As God's love was poured into us, our faith began to grow.

We saw the face of Jesus on everyone at the walk.
The haze of doubt began to lift as we heard talk after talk.

Our tears of joy fell shamelessly as we opened up our hearts.
The baggage we had left behind could fill a zillion carts.

And we did sing and play and shout, as everyone had fun.
And oh, the lights were all around, from far each one had come.

Just like the walk to Emmaus in Luke 24 of gospel old,
Our hearts did burn within us as God's story did unfold.

We felt God's grace and love in ways not felt before.
We saw the Holy Spirit at work, which made us want it more.

So what happens on this walk? It's not easy to explain.
All we know is we've been transformed and we're glad not the same.

No Longer Do I Live for Me

No longer do I live for me; my life is not my own.
I live to bring the Savior's gift to each and every one.
He showered me with love and joy, with grace and people caring,
At Dunklin on my Emmaus walk, where everyone was sharing.

We let down all our defenses and laid our souls so bare.
We received no bit of sorrow, just kind words of loving care.
Our trembling turned to joy as we shared our hidden fears,
As we let go our guilt and shame and shed so many tears!

Look around—oh, look and see we're all the same: God's people in need.
In need of hope and love and grace! Relief from all our sin and greed!
We came in doubt or came in fear. What would this weekend bring?
But soon we learned that rooster song, and other songs to sing.

And did we sing? And did we eat? And did we always have a treat?
But when we heard great talks of God, it was His Word that we did eat!
And how about that sea of lights, all aglow on Saturday night?!
So many faces of Jesus there! What a mighty, mighty sight!

Throughout four days, we grew and grew until we could stand no more.
We realized how empty we were, and how abundantly restored.
Before we left, each one did say what we learned and what we'd do.
Knowing that for Jesus all our fourth days we live for You.

At Dunklin on my Emmaus walk, where everyone was sharing.
God showered me with love and joy, with grace and people caring,
I live to bring the Savior's gift to each and every one.
No longer do I live for me; my life is not my own.

God's Welcome!

Almighty God, He's our guiding light,
Loving us both day and night!
He reaches out to bring us near,
To keep us safe, allay our fear!

But some resist His quiet call,
And wrongly think they cannot fall.
No hell exists, they are so sure,
And doubt His word—'tis Satan's lure!

But be it known God's word is true.
Seek Him out, and He'll find you.
He'll bring relief, peace, love, and joy.
Your guilt and shame He will destroy.

No one's worthy—no, not one!
That's why God sent His precious Son
To pay the price for you and me,
To bear our pain and set us free.

How wonderful our God is!
Salvation plan, His offered kiss!
It shows He cares for everyone,
Unworthiness from us undone!

For God does know no one would seek
Their way to Him, for we are weak.
Our will, though free, it seeks the flesh;
Our minds they can't our hearts refresh.

Until we hear our God's Good News,
We can't have faith His words to muse.
For faith won't come without His words,
For us to hold with silver cords.

At Jesus' name, some men still curse;
Blinded by sin, they think the worst
As they reject God's saving grace,
Care not to know the pain they'll face.

One day God says judgment will come
To punish those who reject the Son.
But to the saints He'll give rewards,
For they believed God's holy words.

So now we ask before that day,
For all your sins did Jesus pay?
Or will it be a sad review,
Regret to know it will be you?

Come to Jesus while there's still time.
Confess; repent; no more you'll pine.
Believe His words; receive His grace;
Abide in joy in heaven's gates.

Eternal life your soul will sing;
All strife destroyed did Jesus bring!
His gift you have; His mercy's true.
Come see your King! He welcomes you!

Amen!

What Do You Think?

What do you think about a thought? Where does a thought begin?
Does it come from God or Satan, or somewhere deep within?

Think way back of bygone days; remember Tom and Jerry.
Recall the times they always fought; they were angry, not once merry.

At times you'd see an angel on the right shoulder of Tom, the cat,
Who would encourage him to do what's right—to eat no mouse or rat.

But speaking into Tom's left ear, the devil would urge him on.
Go fight and kill and eat that mouse; for a cat, that's right, not wrong.

After all, Tom, you're a cat; that's what you were born to do.
Be the best mouser all around; there's no mouse compassion in you.

But the angel would rebut him. He'd urge Tom to be friends in love.
To remember this mouse named Jerry, like him was created from above.

And so the devil and the angel would argue and argue at length,
Until all their strength was gone, and all their energy spent.

Finally, the cat would decide which of the two he'd believe.
Then he'd act accordingly, and his mental struggle relieve.

But how is this story related to finding the source of a thought?
Tom and Jerry's a cartoon; no wisdom from it can be wrought.

Consider our trusted Bible, then. Did not Satan cause Eve to doubt?
Did not God harden Pharaoh's heart and bring him all troubles about?

Are these three stories related? Are they not really the same?
When we call out to our God, was it Him or Satan who came?

So if our faith is not sound, and our life is beginning to sink,
Be careful which thoughts you submit to! What do you really think?

My view is very simple. God's callings are meant for good.
But Satan's intentions are evil; he would hurt us whenever he could.

And his most effective weapon is found in every man.
He fills us with pride and glory, so we trust in ourselves 'cause we can.

We think that we don't need God; we think we did it all on our own.
In this way we're deeply deceived; Satan keeps us from our true home.

So, to whom should you listen? What do you think? Be careful!

MANY OR FEW?

In Matthew, Jesus tells us, our God *"many"* He calls.
But just a *"few"* are chosen to live within His walls.

Are you one of the *many*? How can you be so sure?
Or are you among the *few*? Your cross do you endure?

When our lives go well each day, for God we feel no need.
When tribulation comes our way, we seek help from the Seed.

But God tells us to thank Him in every circumstance—
In good times and in bad times, in mourning and in dance.

When food and drink have filled us, when everything is fine,
When our hearts are warm and fuzzy, do we give God our time?

When God examines our hearts, He knows just what to do.
As we surrender to Him, we've become one of the *few*.

So are you very certain that you are called and chosen?
Or will you come to learn one day your road to hell's been frozen?

Why did you take that loathsome chance and believe there is no hell?
That God's a myth and legend? And from God's grace no one fell?

Was your body unwilling when your mind inside would cry?
Did you not see God's goodness? Or did you just deny?

Did you fight God's calls to you? Did you want to live your way?
Fight man's eternal battle? God's Word to you not sway?

Why, oh why? Did you not hear? God loves you very much!
You heard about His Son, the Christ. Your heart He came to touch.

"God loves us just the way we are," we hear most every day.
But is our own salvation guaranteed in this simple way?

For Jesus died to atone for sins of the entirety of mankind.
He forgives our wicked ways for those of us who find,

Who find Jesus forgives those, who hear His calls for grace!
Whose broken hearts do cry with contriteness on their face!

For Jesus came to save some—those some who trust in Him,
Who know He died in their place and paid for their every sin!

Many are called; *few* are chosen! 'Tis God's salvation plan!
Only our complete surrender removes us from God's ban.

For when we call on Jesus and humbly bow to Him,
He smiles and says, "Come to Me. I no longer see your sin."

It's then you know you're chosen from the *many* left behind.
God's Spirit now resides in you, and to God your soul does bind.

Welcome to the *few*, God's chosen to live with Him.
You're no longer among the *many*; great joy now swirls within.

Share God's love forever more; worship His amazing grace.
Await His promised coming when you'll gaze upon His face.

Praise God you're not a *many*. Praise God you are a *few*.
Praise God it's you He's chosen to grant you life anew.

Psalm of Doubt to Faith

Lord, I come to You in prayer,
Knowing that You're everywhere.
Yet I sometimes have these fears;
My prayers, they do not reach Your ears.

Lord, remove my doubt! I cry.
Give me hope each time I sigh.
Let me know that You are near,
And that I have no need to fear.

Remind me of Your precious words;
Keep me free like all Your birds.
Remind me that You love me so;
Open my eyes that I will know.

Let me feel Your outstretched arms
As they protect me from all harms.
Teach me, Lord, to trust in You,
In all I'll ever think or do.

Lead me on to the water brave;
Knowing life in You is not grave.
I seek You now with all my might,
Yet struggle at times in days of strife.

But still I know without a doubt
I'll see Your face and want to shout.
So hurry, Lord; take me home soon.
This I pray from my silent room.

Somehow I know You'll hear my prayer
As I sing Your praises everywhere.
Thank You, Lord, wherever You are;
Somehow I know You're near, not far.

'Cause from Your word I came to learn;
Your promises are truly firm.
The price was paid by Your own Son,
And offered to each and everyone.

You tell me I'll live eternally
In a room prepared 'specially for me,
Where peace and love and joy abound.
In Jesus only, this is found.

Over and over, You show compassion,
Forgiving sinners of every passion.
You empty them of guilt and shame,
Rejoicing in the Father's name.

And though I think I've sinned too great,
Jesus says, "Come be My mate."
When He sees you, repent your sin.
That is when He says, "Come in."

Believe, not doubt; stand firm in your faith.
Rewards await you at the gate.
Now I live expectantly
For Jesus to come and rapture me.

Thank You, God, for this great news.
No longer must I have to muse.
Now I worship You and wait,
For You to come and complete my faith!

Amen

Psalm of Assurance

Lord, I came to You in faith, knowing that You'd give me grace.
For when I gave my heart to You, of my sin there is no trace.

You showed me that You love me, when Jesus died upon the cross.
You took my heart; I surrendered, but I suffered not a loss.

I won, I won! I'm born again! You chose me; now I sing
Until the day You come for us and eternal life You'll bring.

For when You come, You'll snatch us up into a cloudy sky.
Never again will we face death in that coming by and by.

I know that I can trust our God; every promise He has kept.
Now I wait expectantly; from death, I'm now bereft.

See the smile upon my face, that thankful, joyful demeanor.
From all sin I've been absolved; my soul could be no cleaner.

So who could ever, ever not be giddy with delight,
When our future is assured by the One who is our Light?

Isn't Jesus wonderful to have made us friend and heir?
He's our way, our truth, and life; He's coming to take us there.

He'll take us into His glory to live with Him and reign.
Eternally we'll serve Him and praise His wonderful name!

Thank You! Thank You, Jesus! Thank You, Holy Ghost!
Thank You, Father God! I love You all the most!

BIBLE TALK

A true story of my Bible talking to me!

My Bible spoke to me; I never will forget.
Words from God, Jehovah, they echo in my head.
Simple words of truth my mind shall ever sing
As I live expectantly awaiting my great King!

Early in that autumn morn, my Savior did I hear!
As I held His holy word, the Bible, to my ear.
In a voice as clear as day that soothed my yearning soul,
He spoke the words I'll ne'er forget that shows His mighty role.

"I love you," were His first words; they filled my heart with glee.
"I want you to spend," He said, *"eternity with me."*
Oh, what joy! These precious words Jehovah spoke that fall!
Why would He, our awesome God, speak to me at all?

"Live like Jesus lived," our Father then did say.
These lovely words of wisdom to follow every day!
But God, He was not finished; He spoke to me once more.
"Love one another!" were His words I'd read before.

What a glorious privilege! What an awesome honor,
That my God would speak to me as I sat there in my parlor!
And so I praise my loving God; my faith He has affirmed.
The essence of His being through Jesus we have learned.

Thank You, God! I thank You, God! Through Jesus we believe
That we shall live eternally; from death we've been relieved.
I will always treasure these precious words He said.
And my hope He's set ablaze by Jesus we are led.

My Bible spoke to me; I never will forget.
Words from God, Jehovah, they echo in my head.
Simple words of truth my mind shall ever sing
As I live expectantly awaiting my great King!

RAPTURE THEN

Rapture! Rapture, everywhere! No atheist in sight!
Our waiting time now over, God starts to set things right.

At first we see dead Christians rise from graves, now taking flight.
Then living Christians close behind, all heading for the "Light."

Look closely at those flying; like fire they are bright.
With new eternal bodies, in clouds they will alight.

In the twinkling of an eye, God ends our worldly plight.
Now we'll live eternally in heaven, devoid of fright.

We see our precious Jesus; His face is pure delight.
He's happy to be with us, loves us with all His might.

We marvel at His promise kept; He ended all our fright.
We will serve Him thankfully where there's neither day nor night.

But down below, upon the earth, all saw this awesome sight.
They realized their chance was gone; they now must face the blight.

Then begins God's wrath on earth; Satan's power is at new height.
For seven years, restraint is gone; no pain or suffering will be slight.

Every Jew and nonbeliever who had a holy rite
Which contradicted Jesus—their pain will be so quite.

Will their hardened hearts grow soft and ask Jesus to alight?
Will their aching hearts come to Him in humbleness, contrite?

Beheadings will be found in every land and nation.
Along with plagues, disease, and drought from which there's no vacation.

"Blessed is He who comes, in the name of the Lord," God must hear,
Before Jesus comes to claim His earth in the appointed year.

Then He'll clean all evil from earth for His millennial reign,
And will positively know the faithful, those to Him who came.

So, be ready for the rapture! Avoid your facing the then.
For then salvation's so very painful, until only God knows when.

'Cause what the then man is doing is paying for his own sin—
The sin, which today Jesus offers - to void the then pain through Him.

Come to Jesus today! Confess and repent at the gate.
Accept Jesus' free gift before it is then, and too late!

THANKSGIVING*

Give thanks to the Lord, our Supreme Being.
Let's call upon Him; let's shout and sing.
Tell of His good deeds, great works that He's done.
Glorify His name, our most treasured One.

Seek Him in prayer; search out His presence.
Trust in His promises. Tear down your sin fences.
Humble yourself. Kneel down before Him.
Ask for forgiveness, and He'll let you in.

Into His presence you then will sing.
Forget your old past; new blessings He'll bring.
Oh, how you'll praise Him and worship His name
In great thanksgiving, 'cause His love to you came.

Oh, how you marvel at the glow of His face!
Before your own eyes the source of all grace!
To dwell in great joy you cannot express;
How wondrous you feel, for you God did bless.

Thank You, our Father, for heavenly bliss.
Your gentle caress! Your loving kiss!
Our hope You've fulfilled; our lives now supernal.
Thank You, oh, thank You for new life eternal.

But then we do think, "Who cleaned up our muss?"
How Has our loving God had compassion on us!
And when we recall Jehovah's great Son,
How Jesus paid the price for the wrongs that we'd done!

---

* Inspired by King David's "Song of Thanksgiving" in 1 Chronicles 16:7–13.

Remember His pain, His hideous death!
How He gave His all unto His last breath!
He suffered for us! He atoned for our sin!
Though we can't repay, He still lets us in.

So now we will shout and praise our great King!
Thank Him forever! His praises we'll sing!
We'll thank Him again and again and again.
When will it stop? Never! There's no final when!

Rapture, Return, and Reign

Ever since Jesus' resurrection, Christians for their Master await.
He said He'd return to get His own, for this is our final fate.

He tells us we will meet Him in the clouds high in the sky.
Dead Christians He will raise first; we live ones follow close by.

In the twinkling of an eye, He'll snatch us up so fast.
He'll give us new eternal bodies—ones that will forever last.

We'll live with Him eternally. No pain, no hurt, no fear!
We'll dwell in peace and love and joy; our eyes will shed no tear.

But those left behind are many. Will they know the rapture occurred?
Or will they remain befuddled because this idea seems absurd?

Soon they'll come to realize only true Christians are gone;
The rapture story had come true, and they fell for Satan's con.

How could this awful thing happen? Why didn't they believe?
What future lies before them? Will God their fears relieve?

The sad truth is so bleak; there will be great tribulation,
For seven painful years, there'll be suffering in each nation.

For restraint is gone, and Satan rules; evil torments everyone—
The consequences for selfishness and denying God's great Son!

The time will come when hope is gone; they'll wish that they were dead.
But God prevents that great delight as wrath befalls each head.

But God is great and God is good; He's full of compassion and love.
For when one repents and cries out to Him, He hears from heaven above.

And when He sees our hearts are broken, sincere, and very contrite,
He smiles, and in the Lamb's book our names he then will write.

Then next you'll rest with Jesus Christ 'til the tribulation time does end.
You'll return with Him and His saints; to earth you shall descend.

For Jesus returns, the Bible says, to purge evil in every nation.
And on that day by His mighty power, He ends the tribulation.

In just one day, all hell breaks loose at a place called Armageddon.
Jesus wins the final battle with His voice the conquering weapon.

And so we'll reign a thousand years with Jesus as our King.
Wars and weapons disappear; in peace, we'll live and sing.

Let's celebrate and sing for joy; the time is almost here.
Watch and wait for the Day of Atonement, which ends the jubilee year.

That's when all debts are cancelled and all people to home return.
How wonderful it shall be for us, when God's love in us will burn.

Always remember the three *R*'s: rapture, return, reign!
It's God's process and His promise for the grand eternity we shall gain.

So, praise our God almighty! Thank Him for what He's done!
Prepare to live in glory through His only begotten Son.

Then sing and shout and dance, and praise God who loves us all.
Raise to God the Doxology, which makes us stand so tall.

"Praise God, from whom all blessings flow.
Praise Him, all creatures here below.
Praise Him above, you heavenly host.
Praise Father, Son, and Holy Ghost! Amen!"*

'Tis pleasure to serve our awesome God, the God of love and grace.
Eagerly we wait His call, when then we'll see His face.

Oh, what great expectations! Oh, how our hearts do yearn!
Once we have been raptured home, there's nothing more to learn.

For when we're brought to Jesus, as pure as brand-new snow,
We'll never ever be in want; our God has told us so!

---

* **"The Doxology," text by Thomas Ken.**

PSALM AFTER PSALM, AFTER PSALM, AFTER PSALM

A lament of Ed to the Psalm's Class

Psalm after psalm, after psalm, each day!
We read so many psalms every possible way.

Again and again and again we read
Each psalm until our minds seem to bleed.

Why, oh why, do psalms we read? Why do we strain in vain
As we struggle to understand and ease our mind's pain?

Could these be God's trials and tribulations?
Is it His testing way to jubilation?

For week after week, after week, after week
Do the psalms contain the face we seek?

Torture, testing, reading, resting—our minds, oh, how they ache!
But something happens along the way; our hearts begin to quake!

The light goes on and the fog doth lift.
We find God's words are His precious gift.

Rediscover, we do, what we knew all along:
God's words are to us His precious love song.

Lift us up, Father! Strike up the band!
'Til You hold us in the psalm of Your hand.

So strengthen us, Lord, each day we trudge on!
Reading psalm after psalm, after psalm, after psalm.

ODE TO THE DEATH OF THE *R*'S

The choir did sing so loud and clear!
The words they sang as you'd expect to hear.

But, lo, the leader stopped them short.
"I'm hearing *R*'s; be there none in my court."

R's are not *wohthy* for us to sing.
To our *redeemah* they put a sting

Forevah and *forevah* we shall *heah*
Bureh the *R*'s or live in *feah*!

And so the *choiah* in one *accohd*
Silenced the *R*'s in each *wohd*.

They sing and keep the *R*'s in check.
Did as *they'ah* told! What the heck!

"*Wheah*?" You wonder *wheah* the *R*'s went.
Into the sound system, awaiting voices be sent.

Theah to rejoin *wohrds* from whence they came.
The congregation will *heah* the *R*'s once again.

Oh, how *wondahful*! Oh, how *mahvelous*!
MJ and Cynthia's wisdom, as they pass it to us.

But know this, you *R*'s: your fate is sealed.
Youah shadow of silence is always revealed.

Though we try hard to avoid your great sound,
God gave us minds; that you *R*'s shall abound!

I Too Must Trust and Obey

When God created heaven and earth,
He saw man unruly and his morality dearth.
When God saw this all, He came up with a plan
To save every person, every woman and man.

He sent His Son, Jesus, to die for all sin,
But only for those whose hearts He would win.
To those who believed the Gospel of truth
With a believer's faith, the faith of a Ruth.

But Jesus, He wavered. Must I drink this cup?
When He knew very well, 'twas part of His sup.
"Not my will but thine," He said in agony.
"'Twas Me my Father sent, to die for you and me!

Must I bear this pain of galactic propitiation?
Is no on else worthy to save those of each nation?"
God looked round and said, "'Tis only You can save."
Jesus said reluctantly, "I'll obey," and was brave."

To the cross Jesus went as blood fell from His brow.
No one could save Him; they couldn't see how.
So hang Him they did on a cross very high.
He asked God to forgive them in a voice very dry.

Jesus had obeyed and bore the pain due all sinners.
But in His heart, He knew His believers would be winners.
Believing on Lord Jesus is the only way to life.
For Jesus is our Redeemer; He relieves grief and strife.

Look upon the cross and ask, "What does it really mean?"
Did He, our Lord, give His life for us? Or is this but a dream?
Yes, 'tis true, 'cause our God is great. He forgives and forgets every sin.
He replaces it with peace, love, and mercy in our hearts, very deep within.

But Jesus will only save those whose hearts are broken and contrite,
Who submit completely to Him, who repent and try to live right.
He also tells us if we love Him, we must obey His every command.
He'll forgive and forget our sins. On His promises we'll stand.

How do we know this assertion is true? Where's proof to have us believe?
Listen carefully to my simple words, and one day your sins He'll relieve.
Many saw Jesus crucified and dead, then three days later saw Him alive.
His disciples died believing this. Think they all died for a lie?

Then fifty days later, in the upper room, God's Spirit lit on each one.
They spoke in languages they did not know to Jews from every nation.
They told of God's great glory and aggressively witnessed to all.
Thousands then came to believe in Jesus; they heeded the disciples' call.

Two millennia later, the world honors Jesus, the king.
Knowing Jesus died and arose 'twas an awesome, awesome thing!
AD means Anno Domini in Latin; in English, "in the year of our Lord."
It refers to the years since Jesus was born, as found in God's true word.

When I think of Father, Son, Holy Spirit, and everything that they've done,
My heart explodes with joy and love; I know my heart they've won.
My gratitude is now boundless. Thanksgivings I lift up every day.
Since Jesus trusted and obeyed His Father, I also must trust and obey.

GOD'S HOLY BAND OF THIEVES

God sends thieves into the world to counter Satan's game.
He fills them with great courage when to Jesus sinners came.

For when they heard the gospel and learned that God is good,
They ran to Him and surrendered; they confessed as best they could.

When God looked into their hearts and saw they were sincere,
He smiled and bid them, "Welcome! I'm glad you now are here.

Remember how you feel right now, the joy you have within.
For this is why I send you out to relieve others of their sin.

So listen to me closely; many others need relief.
I'm sending you into the world; I'm making you a thief.

Yes, you heard Me rightly: this job, it seems amiss.
But listen to me closely. In time, you'll feel the bliss.

For Satan now controls lost souls everywhere on the earth.
You must go and steal them back; of their sin, there is no dearth.

Share with them the Gospel and about our God's great love.
When they learn how good He is, they'll seek new life above.

Be strong and be courageous; I'll be with you all the time.
Leave fear and fright behind you. You're bringing back what's Mine.

Yes, you go as holy thieves, God's righteous thieves with power.
It was for such a time as this that I prepared for you this hour.

I send you into restaurants. Go sit where all can see.
Study my word aloud there; it will bring some others to Me.

Sit down. Eat your breakfast. Have a cup of coffee too.
When I see two or more of you, I'm also there with you.

Prepare to feel the bliss as others come to you.
Go steal lost souls from Satan, so they'll feel just like you.

Put aside your shyness; smile, reach out in love.
For you're my holy band of thieves, which I'm guiding from above."

CHRISTMAS GIFT IN JANUARY
Dedicated to my lovely wife, Nita

Thank You, God, for Christmas and the gift of your great Son.
So priceless and eternal, none better could ever come.

But in Your grace, O God of love, You sent a woman fine.
One most caring and loving, like those of the heavenly kind.

You sent her when I needed someone to lend an ear.
But then a relation blossomed, one lasting many a year.

When I recall our wedding and the snow that January day,
An angel God sent down to me dressed in splendid array!

Her smile it set the church aglow, all dressed in glory white!
A dainty hat upon her head, and a bouquet of great delight!

So petite and very lovely was this angel that God sent.
A heart of gold, so full of love, her life to me He lent.

Oh, my heart, how it did soar as she glided slowly down the aisle.
I thanked God that He sent her to share my life for a while.

True love it was that brought us before the Lord that day.
He blessed our sacred marriage so special in every way.

Since then, she's loved me pure; my spirit ever uplift.
Thank You, God, for Nita—My precious Christmas gift.

So remember, God did join us; 'tis true and not a guess.
Jesus is God's greatest gift; but you, my love, are priceless!

CHOIR QUEEN

Dedicated to Cynthia Beam, choir director, First United Methodist Church, Port St. Lucie, Florida

There once was a choir director; her name was Cynthia Beam.
She led our choir throughout nine years and became the choir queen.
She started out a novice, but the Spirit led her on.
She grew into a maestro and earned respect from everyone.

With teachings from an expert—Dr. MJ was her name—
She learned details of the music trade and was never again the same.
Cynthia then taught us notes: wholes, halves, quarters, and eighths.
When to sing and when to rest, and when some notes were mates.

She often would remind us that we're there to sing God's praise.
She'd rescue us from abysmal singing, and great sounds in us she'd raise.
At times when we would practice, her countenance showed some alarm.
How could practice be so awful, but in church sing with great charm?

But regardless how we sang, she kept our spirits high.
She knew the Spirit led our songs from places in the sky.
Cynthia always inspired us; she smiled from ear to ear.
As she led us in God's praises, we sang in tones so clear.

My, how the years have passed since she began to lead!
How we've come to love her as her guidance we did heed.
The time has come to say "So long!" to our leader, oh so fine.
We thank you, and we thank God for all your loving, leading time.

But sad we're not, for we all know in church we'll sing with you,
Praising God in those special ways the ways you taught us to.
We know the Lord has seen and heard the great work you had done,
And He's prepared a room for you, with a choir loft for fun.

THE DOCTOR

Dedicated to Dr. M. J. Montague, pianist and organist, First United Methodist Church, Port St. Lucie, Florida

There once was a music lady; her name was Dr. MJ.
God led her to our church one morn when she was lost and gone astray.
"Is there a doctor in the house?" the music director asked aloud.
"Our piano player is ill. Is there a replacement in the crowd?"

"Yes!" one woman said. "I can play a note or two.
I'd be happy to assist the Lord; I'll do what I can do."
That was many years ago since that fateful Sunday morn.
When God sent us Dr. MJ, her music skills to us adorn.

She fled the snow and cold of that state that's far up north.
She brought her store of music wealth, and on us she poured it forth.
She taught us how to round our mouths and sing from our diaphragm,
To bury *R*s, to stand up tall, and the word "evul" did she ban!

But more than teach, how she could play the piano and organ too!
Her fingers danced and strolled and swooped, 'cross the ivories how they flew!
On top of that, watch her feet: how at the organ they moved with flair.
They moved at times so wonderfully, even better than Fred Astaire!

But life goes on; new paths we take as God gives us a hint.
We gotta slow down, He tells us, or we'll end up just a glint.
MJ, how we'll miss you, but our love for you won't wane,
For we know someday we'll find you in the Music Hall of Fame!

Thank you, MJ, for blessing us with your presence, talent, and love!

DOCTOR JOE

(Dedicated to Dr. Joseph Martin, joint choir director, Jensen Beach, Florida

Doctor Joe is quite the man, and music is his passion.
He comes to lead a rag tag choir in extraordinary fashion.

He has us sing his songs so well, and each member does he amaze.
How does he get that perfect sound in oh so many ways?

He has us synchronize the music he did write;
Through synergy and synthesis has us singing it just right!

And when we do, we all can see he grins from ear to ear.
His eyes light up, his cheeks grow round; his praises we do hear.

What great delight to see him thrilled and hear his words of praise!
But since he's from Frog Level, NC, we oft wonder what he says.

But don't let his accent fool you; this man is razor sharp.
For he's never once confused a piano for a harp.

Yes! He knows all music; he plays just every kind.
His talent is supernal; few on earth like him you'll find.

By his wit and by his charm, each tune in us he molds.
This music man of great renown, each song 'round us enfolds.

So when we come to practice, on his words we love to graze,
Knowing that we'll learn new ways to sing his songs in praise.

He teaches how to own each song, to sing each word with heart.
For it is through our demeanor each song's message we impart.

He tells us 'bout all music and how it fills a void in space.
This simple yet so brilliant fact our minds warmly embrace.

Listen to Joe's music—a gift God daily bestows!
Delighting our hearing senses and touching our very souls!

What shall we say of Dr. Joe and of the beautiful music he creates?
He's blessed by God and worships Him as we approach the pearly gates.

We praise You, God, for sending Joe, who blesses us with Your glory.
And we thank you, Joe, for leading us and being part of your earthly story.

GOD TOUCHED MY HEART

How God touched my heart through intercessory prayer for Susie Martin!

"What just happened?" I ask myself, my eyes awash in tears.
I try to understand my state, for I am void of fears.

All I did was say a prayer for Susie before she went
Into the operating room, where her surgeon had been sent.

Her left hand lay between my two as I began to pray.
She placed her other hand on top in a very gentle way.

With our heads bowed in reverent love, we knew God would be here.
And I began to seek out God with words He would find dear.

I prayed that all would go as planned with not one complication,
That she would heal fast and completely under God's observation.

'Twere just a few simple words I offered to our Lord,
But I knew our awesome God had heard my every word.

For when we said "Amen" I saw her grateful face.
With many tears running down her cheeks, I knew she felt God's grace.

It was then my heart was pierced with a joy I can't explain.
To be with someone touched by God, who heard my prayer and came!

He came and filled her heart with peace in the face of uncertainty.
He gave us both great affirmation that all fears from her did flee.

For Susie's heart was touched by God, Who was with her from the start.
But little did I realize God would also touch *my* heart.

MISS ME ... BUT SMILE WHEN YOU DO
Dedicated to Nita, my lovely wife, should Jesus call me home before you.

This day to you may swell with grief.
My voice thinks not you'll hear.
'Tis a myth, my love, for close I am;
Please, don't shed a tear.

Yes, I came to the door of peace,
And the Lord opened it wide for me.
I entered into that Promised Land,
For my soul is finally set free!

I kneeled before my Master.
He smiled upon my face.
I now enjoy the promised gift,
Eternal life through Jesus' grace!

I bask within His presence
And marvel at life anew.
In perfect love so pure and holy,
With joy and peace I never knew.

Oh, yes! I'm in a better place,
The best place one can be!
A supernal room beyond compare!
The one Jesus prepared for me!

So do not cry that you I left,
Or fret that away I flew.
Remember all our good times.
Miss me ... but smile when you do.

Remember all my stupid puns,
And a clever one or two!
Smile when you see a swimming guck,*
Or drink a dark German brew.

Think of our honeymoon trip, so fine;
Over that large ocean we did go.
The first time ever for me in a plane,

---

* Ed's great niece's word for *duck* when she was three.

50

And the wine chilled in the snow.
And do not forget that big German city
That we passed by but did not see.
Sign after sign read "Ausfart," "Ausfart,"
Which meant "exit" to you, but not to me.

How we laughed at my naiveté
As we drove through snow that night.
When I pulled the emergency cord in the bathroom,
Maids running to our room in fright!

Oh, how you laughed with delight
As I learned things foreign to me.
"Zwie bier, bitte," you taught me to say—
"Two beers, please;" and there they'd be.

And never forget the footprints*
As we waited for the train.
In the lavatory in the station,
And with a smile, out I came.

Think of all the love we shared,
The many places that we went!
The times we consoled our sometimes grief,
Together precious times spent!

Every time you close your eyes
And think of words I said,
Deep within, my voice you'll hear,
Whispers proving I'm really not dead.

I'm in a place to which you'll come
At God's appointed time.
For love never ends in heaven
With our Majesty so sublime.

Yes, I live in profound peace,
Awaiting those I love.
For while I speak so silently,
You'll hear me because of love.

_____

* **Men's urinals had footprints showing where to place your feet before urinating!**

51

Miss me, dear, but make it short.
At the door I wait for you!
Prepare for rapture, your faith fulfilled,
Miss me ... but smile when you do.

Life's journey on earth, each one must take.
Remember—you walked not alone.
Our love we chose, and God did bless
On the path to our heavenly home.

Let your aching heart not cry
When you see the morning dew.
Whenever you remember me,
I'm still right there with you.

Though you may not see me,
Nor my familiar voice do hear,
My presence lies within your heart,
Just beyond your shadow of fear.

So, my love, so far yet near,
Rejoice in God's plan for you!
One day we shall meet again!
'Til then, miss me ... but smile when you do.

LaFontaine once said, "Remembrance is presence in absence,
speech in silence, the ceaseless return of a past happiness."

Nita, I think he was right! "Au Revoir, my love; 'til we meet again."

Your Ed

GET WELL SOON

There once was a lady named Susie Q.
Served bacon and eggs, but not barbeque.

She had a condition not anyone knew
That would frighten both me and you.

So off to the surgeon one day she had gone,
To fix that which somehow had someway gone wrong.

He opened her up her tummy, not swollen,
And found one-third of her colon was stolen.

He was so stunned; he closed her up quick.
Was this the missing link that made her so sick?

But since her heart as normal did tick,
The doctor really didn't give a lick.

"Go home," he said, "for now take it easy.
For in the coming months you'll feel queasy."

But this mystery left him uneasy.
Stealing a colon was very sleazy.

Do not worry or fret, dear Susie.
Your colon is quite a doozie.

I will Google* and I will find a cluezie,
We'll find that sneaky, thieving floozy.

And when we do, I'll put it back.
No colon will you then ever lack.

Get well soon! We'll search and search.
We will not leave you in a lurch.

* Copyrighted

The Decision

Dedicated to Jim Dolan, faithful member of our Emmaus reunion group

Jim was one of our group, the Emmaus reunion team.
Met at Susie Q's each week, sometimes to let off steam.

We talked about faith and God and what we each believed.
Shared our unique stories, and many grievances relieved.

Jim told us all about how at church he loved to cook
Corned beef and cabbage, for which the congregation would look.

On St. Patty's day, Jim said, was that one special delight.
He reveled in cooking this special meal; he made it oh just right.

And don't forget Faith's talent show, when Jimmy danced a jig!
Dressed in drag, his mustache gone; looked great in his new wig.

No one can remember who won the show that day,
But when we saw this side of *her*, there was nothing more to say.

And being from Long Island, Jim loved the New York Yanks.
Could watch them every day, even if he ate just franks.

You seldom saw our Jim without a Yankee cap,
Or a Yankee shirt, or something else like that.

And speaking of baseball caps I must tell you this:
Jim, he always wore a cap and was seldom in remiss.

First time I saw him capless, I knew not who he was.
A bespectacled little fellow whose head was covered with fuzz!

Oh, how we all laughed when I realized it was Jim.
With or without a cap, Jim was always loving within.

Jim loved his family well, praised them every one.
Traveled each year to see them 'cause they were much fun.

And over the years, our Emmaus group became like family to him.
Each Wednesday when we'd meet, you'd feel his love within.

Then sometime over the last few years, Jim's strength began to fade.
He had a myriad of health issues; he grew weak but never afraid.

We prayed him through operations time and time again.
We saw his struggles increasing each time we'd be with him.

And of his last back surgery, no pain did it relieve.
We could see how more and more his body & soul did grieve.

We'd see the bruises and bandages from his most recent falls.
He'd shrug them off like a tough guy, but God did not answer our calls.

Our prayers God heard, we're sure, but not to heal our Jim.
God's wisdom is beyond us, but we still trust in Him.

'Cause one day we shall see Jim alongside Christ, our Lord.
Our hearts will fill with joy and love, though now we hear no word.

So while we loathed Jim's choice—nourishment to deny—
He knew where he was heading; it's we left behind who cry.

We'll always remember Jim as the happy saved soul he is.
Smile each time we think of him, and then blow him a kiss.

Oops! Hold on a sec! Guys, don't blow kisses to guys.
Yes, we'll hug and shake hands, but no Emmaus brother cries.

Well, maybe, just maybe, we'll cry; gone is our beloved brother.
Especially one with a head of fuzz—a fellow like no other.

We miss you, Jim, as we bide our time; here on earth we wait.
Knowing one day we'll reunite just inside God's heavenly gate.

De Colores, Jim! We love you! We'll be with you in God's time.
Until then, we'll remember you fondly, we guys of the Emmaus kind.

Jim's Emmaus Reunion Members over the Years

Mike Overly, Pat Kulikowski, Tom Minch
Jon Arnold, Don Akerberg, Ed Rishko

09/20/98 - 06/13/15

TWINKLE, TWINKLE

Twinkle, twinkle, traffic light;
You are working day and night.

Red means "Stop!"
Green means "Go!"
Yellow means to "Start to slow."

Twinkle, twinkle, traffic light;
You are working day and night.

This terse poem was created for my first grandson, Zachary, when he was about four years old. He sat in his car seat in the back seat of our car on our way to somewhere. It was an instructional poem explaining what traffic light colors meant, and He loved it. How simple!

I Love You, Jacob

I love you, Jacob. Oh, yes, I do.
I don't love any grandson more than you.
When you're not with me, I'm *blue*.
Oh, Jacob, I love you.

This short song was created for my second grandson, Jacob. When he was about four years old, he sat in his car seat on the back seat of our car while we were on our way to preschool. It follows the "I Love You, Jesus" tune we all know.

When Jacob first heard it, he smiled and said, "Sing it again, grandad." I sang it a second time. "Sing it again, grandad." I sang it a third time. And one last time, he said, "Sing it again, grandad!" I did. There was utter silence from the back seat for about ten seconds. Then Jacob asked me in his serious voice, "grandad, when did you turn blue?" Oh, the joy of innocence! That day he learned a metaphor: what it means when someone says he is blue.

ALYCIA'S REDEMPTION*

This married man attracted my attention very strong.
I had an affair with him, though I knew that it was wrong.

With him I'd make a baby; it seemed to me so right.
But when I did get pregnant, my joy turned into fright.

Will my family love me? What will my friends now say?
I feared I'd be rejected. This baby's caused a fray!

"What have I done?" I ask. I'm ashamed and so depressed.
My messiness and strife, can someone from me wrest?

For people frown upon those with child but not a dad.
Will my baby have a life, or be rejected and be sad?

And so I thought to terminate the one within my womb.
But my conscience yelled at me, "Don't let it be tomb!"

Can I take my unborn's life before one breath it takes?
Before one smile it gives me, before a life it makes?

But I decided anyway to save my child and me.
From a life devoid of love, this surely I did see.

I bought that lie which Satan sent, which made me feel so good.
He told me it was good for us! Just do it, because you could!

I went ahead and ended the innocent life inside.
This was the best thing I could do because I was no bride.

I thought that I could live with the turmoil deep inside.
But would my fellow Christians forgive this sin so wide?

But praise God, for He spoke to me: "Alycia, I still love you.
About the guilt and shame you have, I'll tell you what to do.

---

* **Inspired by a "godfruits.tv" video entitled Abortion Story//Alycia at <u>http://www.godfruits.tv/wom-an-finds-jesus-after-abortion/?ref=11&utm_source=getresponse&utm_medium=email&utm_campaign=in-fo_870035&utm_content=Nothing+Could+Save+Her+From+The+Regret+Of+Abortion+Until+She+-Found+Jesus</u>. Because all facts about this video's context are unknown, poetic license was used.**

Regardless that you knew it was sinful from the start,
Earnestly confess, repent! I'll unburden your heavy heart.

I'll take from you the whirlwind of your aching, troubled mind.
I'll eradicate the hopelessness; in you, no more you'll find."

So to God I gave my broken and contrite heart in deep faith.
He forgave me, and then He smiled; my praises can no more wait.

I thanked Him and praised Him, with my heart all fresh and clean!
I'd been emptied of my sinfulness; there's no sin in me to glean.

My heart is all aglow! All stain of sin is gone!
Only God could do this; He is the only One.

My awesome God has taught me that He's abounding in compassion.
He knows that we all sin at times; we're wrought with earthly passion.

From murder, abortion, and all sin, our Lord can set us free.
Yes, our sins seem unforgiveable, but our God is full of mercy!

So accept the goodness of our God, Who brings you calm and peace.
Give your broken heart to Him; from your sins He'll then release.

Know that Jesus loves you. He wants no one to perish.
Accept Him as your Lord, and you then He will cherish.

Never give up on our great God; He's like a tree with many branches.
'Cause He never gives up on you; He gives you many chances.

So if you are uncertain, and you begin to scream,
Remember that God loves you; your soul He will redeem.

SHADOW OF DEATH

The Truck of Death, it barrels down,
That narrow road of life.
It speeds so fast toward each of us,
Brings fear and lots of strife.

A prod that makes us understand
The danger it might bring
To those who stand within its path;
There's death and its great sting.

But also notice, along with it,
Goes the Shadow of Death in stride.
Looking not so ominous,
Mere darkness along one side.

For as the sun shines on the truck,
It illuminates it so brightly.
But opposite the sunny side,
The Shadow of Death travels lightly.

So when you see that Truck of Death
Approach at breakneck speed,
A serious choice you must make—
And you must make it indeed!

Will you challenge four tons of steel?
Will you stay in its lane of travel?
Or will you move onto the shoulder
And hope your life won't unravel?

For if the truck comes and strikes you hard,
You most certainly will die.
But if the *shadow* runs over you,
You will live! Do you know why?

Of course we know the answer.
When two solid bodies collide,
The lesser will be overcome.
The body dies; the truck survives.

But the *shadow* will not hurt you.
It's nothing but lack of light!
When it strikes you at full strength,
There's no reason for any fright.

Now, using this analogy,
I posit something new.
Life is either a truck or a shadow;
It depends on your point of view.

To unbelievers, life's a truck:
It runs you down, and you are dead.
But to Christians, life's a *shadow*
With an afterlife instead!

We Christians know the truth;
We know real life is eternal.
God gave us souls at conception;
They'll return to Him supernal.

No, we Christians are not afraid
That our earthly bodies die.
God will give us new, perfect ones
To live with Him on high.

So what am I truly saying?
Are you afraid of your last breath?
Afraid the Truck of Death will hit you,
And not the Shadow of Death?

Remember the shadow lacks substance;
It can't hurt you in any way.
Avoid the truck, seek the shadow.
"Come to Jesus now," I say.

For when you become a Christian,
Your future is then assured.
You'll live with Jesus forever,
Kept alive by His very word.

So, do not fear that Truck of Death;
Let it take away your breath.
Then you'll laugh and understand
They were both just a Shadow of Death.

METHODIST'S FOOD
From Your Disciple III Class of 2014–2015

Methodists is our name; faith and food is our game.
On casseroles we all feast in our Lord Jesus' name.

At first we greet and hug; next we gather to eat.
Our bodies we must feed to battle all deceit.

Then we sit en masse and eat our share of chow.
We eat and drink 'til full, then eat some more somehow.

But 'tis not food we seek; it's our God's holy word.
As we read the Bible, we embrace each verse we heard.

Oh! Give us more and more until we're full and done.
Until we cannot resist, and go when He says, "Come."

For from the cup we drink the gift offered each one,
Which leads to life eternal when trusting in the Son.

'Cause as we're born again, our souls take on new life.
Then we begin to live to help end other's strife.

We live like Jesus lived; we eat "new" food like Him.
To do the will of God, and to lead more souls from sin!

For Jesus has unique food: to obey the Father's will.
We Methodists believe this; on God's words we seek our fill.

Our casseroles are blessed; in Jesus' name they all went.
To disciples who are called, and apostles who are sent.

So next you see a dish, a casserole so fine,
Remember Jesus' food is the best on which to dine.

FOOD FROM GOD

Read God's Holy Bible. Treasure His commands.
Cry out for discernment! Seek to understand!
Then the God of heaven, His fear you'll come to know.
For the Lord gives wisdom to save you from your foe.
God is love. God is life. He gives you wisdom; ends your strife.
Remember God is in control! He heals your heart and saves your soul.

Never forget, dear brethren, God forgives our every sin.
He loves you, and He wants you to spend eternity with Him.
He wants you to love each other and to live like Jesus lived.
Read and heed His Word each day; by His promises be not grieved.

Scripture tells us Jesus said, "Man does not live by bread alone,"
But by God's every word, beginning with those etched in stone.
He also has a different food—the kind you do not eat.
The kind you're likely unaware; it's like no other treat!
He said to His disciples after the woman at the well had left,
His food is to *do the will of God,* and from nothing be bereft.

So open up your Bible, and God's holy words do read.
He'll comfort you and guide you into everything you need.
When you're low and feeling weak, you now know where to find
Relief from your every sorrow: through God's blessed words so kind.
What wonderful food God does provide! With joyful hope, we are filled!
For by His every word we live! Lifted up, saved, and thrilled!

Feast upon God's banquet spread, and ponder His words as we look.
Be filled with His promised hope and love, found in His precious book.

Read God's Holy Bible; treasure His commands.
Cry out for discernment; seek to understand.!
Then the God of heaven, His fear you'll come to know.
For the Lord gives wisdom, wise words with which you grow.

And always remember God loves you.
He'll never leave you or forsake you.
The Spirit says, "Come!" Jesus says, "Come!"
The Bible shows you which way to run!

To Jesus!

BOTTOMLESS PIT

Where, oh where is the bottomless pit?
Where, oh where can it be?
The answer is very simple,
But you must think logically.

When you dig a shallow pit,
Climb out, and then look down,
You see the bottom as clear as day;
You smile and do not frown.

But dig the pit as far as you can.
You end up on the other side—
Of earth, that is, and what do you see?
You see the sky, and then you cried.

You cried because you were confused.
You dug down but then dug up,
Not knowing somewhere along the way,
Your down turned into up.

What happened? 'Tis a puzzlement!
But of yourself you must ask this:
"Where, within our planet earth,
Looking up you cannot miss?"

Don't you know that from earth's center,
Any way you look is up?
The "bottom" of the pit disappears,
And "down" ends there so abrupt.

Now, by this simple illustration
Whose logic is very clear,
The bottomless pit lies at earth's center;
It is, in fact, that near.

"Not true," you think, and then you ask,
"What does God say about this place?"
He tells us souls go *down* to the pit,
So it can't be in outer space!

And scripture is written for people
Who live *upon* earth everywhere.
To think it refers to some other place
Seems evasive with no logic that's fair.

As Christians we believe in angels;
We believe in heaven and hell.
We believe in new life eternal;
We believe in miracles as well.

All of this seems unbelievable
As we live by faith, not wit,
And if you believe all of scripture is true,
You know where to find the bottomless pit.

Our Lawless, Lawful Man

Dedicated to Jim Lawless, deceased choir member, First United
Methodist Church, Port St. Lucie, Florida

Jim Lawless was a lawful man; a lawful man was he.
From Hoboken did he come. From him criminals would flee.

For Jim once was a detective all around the New York City.
He sent many crooks to prison who thought they were clever and witty.

That was many years ago when Jim did dangerous work.
He once was even shot at by thieves, and this was not a quirk.

Then Jim and his wife, Marilyn, joined the choir at our church.
They sang to praise and glorify God like lovebirds on a perch.

Once I asked Jim what he'd done in his younger days.
He told of some of his exploits of crooks and their evil ways.

I asked if he used to carry a gun, and with it, what did he do?
He turned and smiled and replied, "What do you mean, used to?"

What a shock I got that night as we sang words to each beat.
Surely he knew God's in control, and he need not pack his heat.

No, I never saw his gun, but 'tis fascinating to tell
How Jim's life was interesting, and that he sang so well.

I also understand that Jim was our mayor years ago.
Another important public job, as everyone did know.

Our Jim had touched so many lives in many different ways,
But serving God in the choir, he did many years and days.

Today we say "Au revoir, dear Jim." We know we'll see you again,
At heaven's gate with our Lord at a time only He knows when.

HANDOUTS

An Acrostic: "Handouts of Rad Orlandi," our beloved Bible study teacher

"_H_andout" is a special word, one that Rad embraces!
_A_lways has them in his hands! Looks for smiles on all our faces!

_N_ever ending, always seeking more to give each class!
_D_oubt we'll ever see the day that we will see his last.

_O_ut of nowhere, he will glean something we can't do without.
_U_nder rocks and in the sand, from these his handouts sprout.

_T_hink about that barren day when no handouts he'd give.
_S_huddering before us sheepishly—lame excuses, "Will _we_ live?"

_O_h, how we loved each of them despite what we may claim.
_F_or God created handouts for Rad, for they bear his name.

_R_each into the clouds so high; Rad's handouts you'll find there.
_A_nd all throughout the BLC, they lie in every chair.

_D_o not think you'll hide from them, nor from them can you run.
_O_h, each one we do embrace and let him think they're fun.

_R_emember the altar of handouts and the trees of sacrifice,
_L_aid there to teach God's lessons for us people and church mice.

_A_lways, always, always; we should always beg for more.
_N_ever will Rad disappoint us; for him, no handout's a bore.

'_D_is is now the end, the time to finish up.
_I_t's time for one last handout before our session's up.

So next you see a handout in his hands he holds with glee,
Think of this acrostic: "Handouts of Rad Orlandi."

Thank you, Rad, for leading us these past thirty-two weeks!

STOP CELEBRATING SIN

Oh, how we have fallen! God's grace from us is gone.
We worship Him no longer, as we did at nation's dawn.
America was founded so men could freely pray.
But now we're told "Be silent!" God's words we should not say.

At first America shunned all sin, but today we celebrate
Things that God said "No!" to, some shout and say, "It's great!"
See our daily paper; it highlights this very fact.
Same sex marriage is praised, but God's approval it does lack.

Oh, how we have fallen! For God's marriage, there's no room.
Troubles all around us! Are these signs of pending doom?
When to God we do return, His grace He'll then restore!
But as we celebrate much sin, He tolerates us no more.

Why do we murder those in the womb and think that God approves?
Why do we butcher and sell their parts? This also our God loathes.
Why do many movies and shows spew God's name in vain?
Do we think God sees this not and from us punishment refrain?

Curse words and profanities are heard almost everywhere.
God is dead or doesn't exist, by these reasons many swear.
'Cause if they're right that God is gone, or God is just a myth,
Then everything is permissible to whomever we are with.

And if no godly rules exist by which we are to live,
Then no one's ever wrong; there's no punishment to give.
So look within our churches and ask them, "What is sin?"
Do they quote the Bible, or are their answers from within?

Look across our nation, once God's magnificent jewel.
All peoples came to live here because so few were cruel.
They came to worship freely in the land of God's great bounty.
They lived as God prescribed and fed on God's word plenty.

People flocked from 'round the world. They came to live! They dreamed
To come and start their lives anew in the country of the redeemed!
For the Gospel was the solid rock upon which life here was built.
On freedom, love, and worship of God, no dreams would ever wilt.

Have we today forgotten that we only stand by God's grace?
Have pastors, priests, ministers, and rabbis failed to keep the pace?
Have they gradually shied away from and tolerated sin after sin?
Have they warned not of a living hell, which one day we may be cast in?

Have they forgotten Toqueville's words as to why the US is great?
That he's the one who noticed Americans' faith brought us good fate?
For Toqueville said, "America is great, because she is good.
If America ceases to be good, America will cease to be great."

Ponder these insightful words; think very hard and long.
For it is our faith in God that makes America strong.
And when we're strong and faithful, and love our neighbors fine,
We generously give and share God's bounty on which all dine.

Harken, take a look around! See the ills in the USA.
Furgeson, Baltimore, New York, Detroit with riots, unrest, and decay.
Why do we see citizens and police fight in their own community?
If all were true brothers and sisters in Christ, we'd have peace and unity.

Oh, how we have fallen! God's grace from us seems gone.
We worship Him no longer, as we did at nation's dawn.
America was founded so men could freely pray.
But now we're told "Be silent!" God's words we should not say.

Will we continue to celebrate sin? Or will we to God return?
Will we call sin what it really is? When will our clergy learn?
Remember—we fight a spiritual battle against Satan and every demon!
Be strong and stand up for God, for His Son gave us great reason!

Read God's Holy Bible; treasure His commands.
Cry out for discernment; seek to understand.
Then the God of heaven, His fear we'll come to know.
For the Lord gives wisdom to save us from our foe.

God tells us if we love Him, then His commands we should obey.
He tells what every sin is that we must live His way.
But somehow all God's people are preached less than the truth.
Has Satan deceived our clergy? Have they broken from the root?

Has their intellectual prowess clouded their biblical view?
Longing to gain more converts, have they strayed from what is true?
Why not let all sinners join Christian congregations?
Isn't that what God tells us: to save sinners in all the nations?

"Yes," they say, this is God's will: to bring all sinners to Him.
Let us fellowship with everyone, regardless of their sin.
And so it went for many years; unrepentant sinners worshiped alongside saints.
But something happened along the way: our minds were filled with taints.

Weekly sermons seemed to be bent, a distortion of God's true word.
We're told God's word is not absolute—a message that's so absurd.
God tells us what human behavior is acceptable and what is not.
And as our creator and sustainer, we must obey Him or we will rot.

"Do not murder," our God commands! "Taking life, this is My job."
But of more than sixty million unborn, our society their lives did rob.
Having sex out side of marriage in our nation once was unlawful.
Now it's celebrated throughout the land; it's no longer deemed so awful.

God says marriage has always been between one man and woman.
He blessed it as a lifelong bond—is not this a holy omen?
The Supreme Court redefined marriage as two men or two women too.
Have we voided God's command? Has Satan deceived them and you?

If this new marriage definition were to be accepted by one and all,
Eventually our society would vanish; lacking babies, all nations would fall.
People know all this is true and that God knows the future ahead.
'Cause when our nation defies its God, they're no longer living but living dead.

Read God's Holy Bible; treasure His commands.
Cry out for discernment; seek to understand.
Then the God of heaven, His fear we'll come to know.
For the Lord gives wisdom to save us from our foe.

When will our clergy realize repentance of sin must be sought,
Before non-believers submit to Christ and into His presence be brought?
For only contrite, repentant sinners are accepted by Jesus, our King.
Before He sends them the Spirit, and their own spirits then loudly sing!

No clergy should be a coward, but courageously God's truth preach
That Jesus Christ died for all man's sins, and how salvation one can reach.
To accept unrepentant sinners as members in God's holy church
Is to disobey the holiness of God, for nothing unclean will He touch.

Gay marriage, abortion, illicit sex, cursing, swearing, lies!
Divorce, deception, and incest are all things that God decries!
He loathes these sins and more; He hurts when they are done.
But still the hounds of heaven pursue us, each and every one.

Yes, our God wants none to perish. He's gracious and forgiving!
He yearns us all to turn from sin, and brings us life worth living.
Then comes the time when we realize salvation we can't earn;
We must humble ourselves, surrender to God, and from our sin then turn.

"Love covers a multitude of sins," some will quote our God so clearly.
And they will argue that's enough to get us to God so dearly.
But nowhere in God's word has He given us such a story:
That anything unclean or impure can enter into His glory.

So, clergy, lift your heads high. Boldly preach what is right!
'Cause knowing you're on God's side, you'll win every fight.
Let's celebrate God's victory through Jesus He did win,
Let's stop slanted preaching. Let's stop celebrating sin!

One Bible verse explicitly tells nations how to make their countries prosper. It is 2 Chronicles 7:14. "If my people, which are called by my name, shall humble themselves, and pray, and seek my face, and turn from their wicked ways; then I will hear from heaven, and will forgive their sin, and will heal their land"

(The Scofield Bible).

YOUR DECISION

God exists and loves us all; He wants no one to perish.
He gave us simple rules to live—all rules that we should cherish.

But when we show disdain for them, tribulation our way He'll send,
Until we learn to come to Him, to repent, and us He'd mend.

His grace He sends when we confess and turn from our wicked ways.
When He sees our hearts sincere, He prepares for us new days!

New days in love and peace and joy sends His Spirit into our hearts.
He gives us new beginnings, brand-new lives, and brand-new starts.

He then forgets our every sin, makes us pure as new-fallen snow.
He leads us to read His Gospel; into Jesus' likeness we'll then grow.

The rewards for trusting in Jesus are life eternal, replete with love!
Joy and happiness evermore God willingly bestows from above!

This is God's glorious promise; it's one that He offers to all.
Every promise He has kept; He grants mercy that none might fall.

But if we reject God's offer, we'll suffer for sins that we did.
Nowhere from God can you hide; not one thing from God can be hid.

But fall we will if from Him we turn, for every sin payment is due.
That's why He sent His only Son to pay all debt for me and you.

The punishment for sin is sure; it's eternal and will never end.
That's why God keeps calling us; He wants us to hell not send.

Only two choices exist; one decision we cannot eschew.
So did Jesus pay for your sins? Or will it one day be you?

Despair not, or think you're doomed if to Jesus you have not yet come.
Do it now before your last breath, when your fate is then sealed and done.

Remember Jesus loves you; He wants you to live with Him,
Open your heart, hear His call! Ask Him, and He'll come in.

Afterword

I shared with my readers the experiences I had with the living God of creation, Jehovah. I offer no physical evidence; there is none. There is nothing but my testimonies. There is nothing but the poems I wrote. I contend they are not of my doing, but that of the Holy Spirit of God. They are Holy Spirit driven. I was merely a willing scribe, an instrument of God's glory. This continues to this day. Hallelujah! In fact, I've also written and composed my first song! So cool!

When I reflect on God, life, and eternity, I cannot help but feel, like the ancient biblical writers, that what I wrote or composed was from God. The final versions of the poems that I wrote did not vary significantly from the original drafts. The words are godly words of love, hope, comfort, and faith; they are biblically accurate, as far as I can determine. They are words to help make one's life more joyful, hopeful, peaceful, certain, and secure about one's eternity. I wholeheartedly believe the contents of this book contain God's truths, especially His truth as God revealed through my life. It's a truth that as a born-again Christian, I cannot stop sharing with anyone and everyone in order to make disciples for Jesus Christ.

What is this truth? It is what you've heard your entire life. It is the Gospel of Jesus Christ! It is the good news—no, the great news: that Jesus Christ grants eternal life. He freely offers it to those who believe He is the Son of God, He died for their sins, and they are willing to die for this belief. But hidden throughout the Bible, in plain view, God also tells us He loves us, He wants us to spend eternity with Him, we should love God and one another, we should live like Jesus lived, we should confess our sins and repent, and He is waiting for us to come to Him. He is now waiting for every one of us with outstretched arms.

And if God would pass such godly wisdom to me, He can certainly pass it to you too. I am nobody special. I am neither especially smart nor dumb. I come from a poor, working-class Roman Catholic environment. My dad was a coal miner and then a parts transporter; my mom was a seamstress and homemaker. Hmm! This kind of reminds me of the low societal status of Jesus' disciples and followers.

I write this in anticipation that, in my humble opinion, the rapture will occur soon. Many, if not most, will disagree with this perspective, but I strongly urge readers to surrender to Jesus Christ before the rapture. Whoever is left behind must endure some, if not all, of the seven-year tribulation period of pain and suffering, before Jesus returns to earth and starts the battle of Armageddon.

For those readers who are biblical scholars, these poems follow the concepts, beliefs, and patterns contained in the book *Charting the End Times*, by Tim LaHaye and Thomas Ice. Their book is the only one I've read that completely aligns with my thoughts and beliefs, which I've learned during eighteen years of intense personal study and research of the Bible.

Let me summarize my beliefs: Jesus is the Son of God; He is God incarnate. He was born, died, resurrected, and translated into heaven. He will come again (soon) to rapture those who believe in Him (all true Christians, both alive and physically dead) to be with Him forever. He will do this just prior to, or simultaneously with, the beginning of the seven-year tribulation. This is the time when God will withdraw His restraint of sin, and the people on earth will experience seven years of sin, lawlessness, pain, and untold suffering. At the end of this tribulation, Jesus Christ and His saints will return to earth and defeat Satan and his followers at the Battle of Armageddon. The Beast and False Prophet will be cast into hell. The souls of the physically dead non-believers will be cast into the bottomless pit (Sheol) to await judgment day, which is at the end of Jesus' thousand-year reign (the millennium).

Lastly, Satan will then be cast into the bottomless pit during the millennium, when he would be released one last time to lead a final rebellion against Jesus. Jesus will win, and Satan will be cast into hell. His followers and all other non-believers in the pit will be brought before Jesus. Then Jesus will judge each soul, pronounce punishment, and cast them into hell, where the fire is never quenched. He will annihilate the existing heaven and earth and create new ones. It is here in which the saved will live eternally with the God the Father, Jesus the Son, and the Holy Spirit in love, joy, peace, and happiness.

Finally, if this summary repulses you or angers you, or intrigues you, don't trust in my views and perceptions of the Bible and what my poems present. Search it out for yourself. No one is damned to hell until his last breath has been taken and he has not accepted Jesus as his Lord and Savior. And because one can only be saved from hell when they realize how good God is (Rom. 2:4), I suggest you also listen to William Shakespeare, who wrote, "This above all: to thine own self be true." That is, don't deceive yourself! Your future is in your hands. But remember no matter how bad you think you think you are or have been, God forgives those who call on Him for help—always. Your future is not finalized, if you are reading this book. Tarry not; time is short. I believe the rapture is near. You may doubt my words, but don't doubt God's words. Accept His free gift. He offers eternal life with Him to avoid eternal suffering without Him. The choice is yours.

May God guide you into His presence and salvation, in Jesus' name!

Printed in the United States
By Bookmasters